© Rudy Gelenter

About the Author

John Baxter, who gives literary walking tours through Paris, is an acclaimed memoirist, film critic, and biographer. He has lived in Paris for twenty years and gained an intimate knowledge of the city and its history, particularly of the expatriate artists who lived there during the twentieth century. His books include the memoirs *Immoveable Feast: A Paris Christmas* and *We'll Always Have Paris*, both available from Harper Perennial. A native of Australia, he lives with his wife and daughter in Paris, in the same building Sylvia Beach called home.

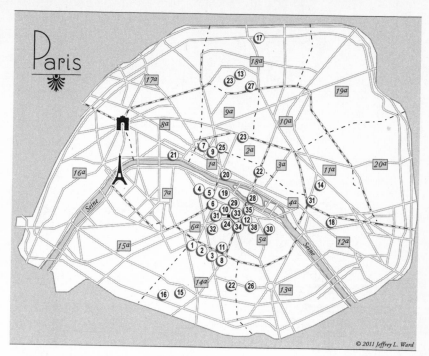

Paris

© 2011 Jeffrey L. Ward

CAFÉS AND RESTAURANTS

1. La Coupole
2. La Rotonde
3. Le Dôme
4. Les Deux Magots
5. Café Flore
6. Brasserie Lipp
7. The Ritz Hotel
8. Dingo Bar (now Auberge de Venise)
9. Harry's Bar
10. Les Editeurs
11. Closerie des Lilas
12. Le Balzar
13. Au Lapin Agile
14. La Fée Verte

MARKETS

15. Porte de Vanves (antiques)
16. Rue Brancion (old books)
17. Porte de Clignancourt (antiques)
18. Marché d'Aligre (food)

ART AND PAINTING

19. Rue Mazarine
20. The Louvre
21. Le Grand Palais
22. Centre Pompidou

SIGHTS

23. The Catacombs
24. The Passages (arcades)
25. Luxembourg Gardens
26. The Opera Garnier
27. La Santé Prison
28. Sacré-Coeur Cathedral
29. Notre Dame Cathedral
30. Cour de Commerce St. Andre
31. Place de la Bastille

LITERARY SITES

32. Ernest Hemingway's apartment (74 Rue Cardinal Lemoine)
33. Ernest Hemingway's apartment (#6 Rue Ferou)
34. Gertrude Stein's apartment
35. Rue de l'Odéon (Sylvia Beach's apartment)
36. Old Shakespeare and Company bookshop
37. New Shakespeare and Company bookshop
38. The Panthéon (burial site of Voltaire, Rousseau, and Zola)

The
Most Beautiful Walk
in
the World

· A PEDESTRIAN IN PARIS ·

John Baxter

HARPER ◉ PERENNIAL

NEW YORK • LONDON • TORONTO • SYDNEY • NEW DELHI • AUCKLAND

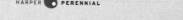

HARPER ● PERENNIAL

THE MOST BEAUTIFUL WALK IN THE WORLD. Copyright © 2011 by John Baxter.
All rights reserved. Printed in the United States of America. No part of this
book may be used or reproduced in any manner whatsoever without written
permission except in the case of brief quotations embodied in critical articles
and reviews. For information address HarperCollins Publishers, 10 East 53rd
Street, New York, NY 10022.

HarperCollins books may be purchased for educational, business, or sales
promotional use. For information please write: Special Markets Department,
HarperCollins Publishers, 10 East 53rd Street, New York, NY 10022.

FIRST EDITION

Map on page iii © Jeffrey L. Ward
Designed by Jennifer Daddio / Bookmark Design & Media Inc.

Library of Congress Cataloging-in-Publication Data

Baxter, John
    The most beautiful walk in the world : a pedestrian in Paris /
John Baxter. — 1st ed.
        p. cm.
    ISBN 978-0-06-199854-6 (pbk.)
    1. Paris (France)—Description and travel. 2. Walking—France—
Paris. 3. Baxter, John, 1939—Travel—France—Paris. 4. Paris (France)—
Social life and customs. I. Title.

DC707.B39 2011
914.404'84—dc22   2010046259

11 12 13 14 15 OV/RRD 10 9 8 7 6 5 4 3 2 1

FOR

Marie-Dominique

AND

Louise,

WORTH WALKING FOR.

We cannot tarry here,

We must march my darlings

—WALT WHITMAN, *PIONEERS, O PIONEERS*

· Contents ·

Contents

Contents

✳ The Most Beautiful Walk in the World ✳

To Walk the Walk

*Nobody has yet found a better way to travel slowly than
to walk. It requires two legs; nothing more. Want to go
faster? Don't bother walking—roll, slide or fly:
don't walk. But once you are walking, it's not
performance that counts but the intensity of the sky,
the splendour of the landscape. Walking is not a sport.*

CHARLES GROS, *Walking: A Philosophy*

$\mathcal{E}$very day, heading down rue de l'Odéon toward
Café Danton on the corner of boulevard Saint-
Germain or toward the market on rue Buci, I pass them.

The walkers.

Not all are walking, however. They'd *like* to be—
but their stroll around Paris isn't working out as they
hoped.

Uncertain, they loiter at the foot of our street, at the
corner of boulevard Saint-Germain, one of the busi-

est on this side of the Seine. Couples, usually, they're dressed in the seasonal variation of what is almost a uniform—beige raincoat or jacket, cotton or corduroy pants, and sensible shoes. Huddling over a folded map or guidebook, they look up and around every few seconds, hopeful that the street signs and architecture will have transformed themselves into something more like Brooklyn or Brentwood or Birmingham.

Sometimes they appear in groups. We see a lot of these because our street, rue de l'Odéon, is to literature what Yankee Stadium is to baseball and Lord's is to cricket. At no. 12, Sylvia Beach ran Shakespeare and Company, the English-language bookshop that published James Joyce's *Ulysses.* Sylvia and her companion, Adrienne Monnier, lived in our building at no. 18. Joyce visited them there often. So did Scott and Zelda Fitzgerald, Gertrude Stein and Alice B. Toklas, and of course Ernest Hemingway.

Most days, when I step out of the building, a group stands on the opposite sidewalk while someone lectures them in any one of a dozen languages about the history of our street. They regard me with curiosity, even respect. But often I feel like a fraud. Instead of thinking lofty literary thoughts, I'm compiling my shopping list. *Eggs, onions, a baguette...*

After that, they set off again, a straggling column, following the guide's flag or, in bad weather, her umbrella. Few take their eyes off this object. They've learned that Paris for the pedestrian is both fascinating and deceptive. What if they did pause—to browse that basket of books outside *une librairie,* or take a closer look at a dress in the window of a boutique? The tour might turn a corner, disappearing from sight, casting them adrift in this baffling town. They would be forced to buttonhole a passing Parisian and stammer, "Excusez-moi, monsieur, mais . . . parlez-vous Anglais?" Or worse, surrender to the mysteries of *le métro.* A few lost souls are always hovering at the entrance to the Odéon station. Staring up at the green serpentine art nouveau curlicues of Hector Guimard's cast-iron archway, they may read *Metropolitain* but they *see* what Dante saw over the gate to hell: "Abandon hope all ye who enter here."

What most frustrates the visitor walking in Paris is the presence all around of others who share none of their hesitation. Confident, casual, the locals breeze past, as careless as birds in a tree. For them, the métro holds no terrors. They know exactly when to pause as a bus roars by on what appears to be the wrong side of the road. They make abrupt turns into alleys, at the foot of which one glimpses the most interesting-looking little market. . .

How do they *know*?

Well, this is their habitat, their *quartier*, as familiar to them as their own living room. Because that's how Parisians regard the city—as an extension of their homes. The concept of public space doesn't exist here. People don't step out of their front door into their car, then drive across town to the office or some air-conditioned mall. No Parisian drives around Paris. A few cycle. Others take the métro or a bus, but most walk. Paris belongs to its *piétons*—the pedestrians. One goes naturally *à pied*—on foot. And it's only on foot that you discover its richness and variety. As another out-of-town Paris lover, the writer Edmund White, says in his elegant little book *The Flaneur*, "Paris is a world meant to be seen by the walker alone, for only the pace of strolling can take in all the rich (if muted) detail."

Another writer, Adam Gopnik, calls a stroll down rue de Seine, just around the corner from our apartment, "the most beautiful walk in the world." And so it is—for him. But every Parisian, and everyone who comes to know Paris, discovers his or her own "most beautiful walk." A walk is not a parade or a race. It's a succession of instants, any one of which can illuminate a lifetime. What about the glance, the scent, the glimpse, the way the light just falls . . . the "beautiful" part? No tour guide or guidebook tells you that. Prepared itineraries remind me of those PHOTO POINT signs at Disneyland. Yes, that angle gives you an attractive picture. But why not just buy a postcard?

Nor is there a single Paris. The city exists as a blank page on which each person scribbles what the French call a *griffe*—literally "a claw" but more precisely a signature; a choice of favorite cafés, shops, parks, and the routes that link them. "I discovered that Paris did not exist," wrote Colette on her arrival from the country. "It was no more than a cluster of provinces held together by the most tenuous of threads. There was nothing to prevent me from reconstructing my own province or any other my imagination should choose to fix in outline."

In a way that isn't possible with London or New York or Berlin, one can speak of "Colette's Paris" or "Hemingway's Paris" or "Scott Fitzgerald's Paris," or your own Paris. We all go through a similar process: finding the only café, the perfect park, the loveliest view, the most beautiful walk.

Nobody can say precisely which they will be. But maybe my experiences of a year of walking in Paris will suggest how and where you might start to find the succession of arrivals and departures that leaves one with memories that can never be erased, the moments one recounts all one's life, prefaced by the words, "I remember . . . once . . . in Paris . . ."

Walk with me.

'Walking Backwards for Christmas'

I'm walking backwards for Christmas,
Across the Irish Sea,
I'm walking backwards for Christmas,
It's the only thing for me.

I've tried walking sideways,
And walking to the front,
But people just look at me,
And say it's a publicity stunt.

SPIKE MILLIGAN, 1956

*M*y first memorable walk of the year came both early and without notice. To be precise, at 3:00 p.m. on Christmas Eve.

Paris under snow

Although, after eating and sex, walking is Paris's preferred activity, it is *never* practiced on Christmas Eve. The hostility to being on foot on December 24 is reflected in the national rejection of Father Christmas. Traditionally, it's not *Père Noël* but the baby Jesus who distributes gifts, and he doesn't need to trudge around as I was about to do, in parka, gloves, fur hat, and insulated boots.

Outside, the temperature hovered around zero. Snow had ceased to fall, but an even gray tone in the sky promised more soon. One could almost hear the crackle as slush hardened into ice. Not that the risk of slippery sidewalks concerned us. Any walking that evening would begin at our front door and end a few meters away at the car parked at the curb. After that, we'd be on the freeway, plowed and gritted for the annual migration. Like Thanksgiving in the United States, Christmas was the time for bonding, for renewal, for reconciliation. *Nobody* stayed in Paris for Christmas.

For the last month, I'd been planning and preparing for Christmas, and in particular for the family dinner.

When I married my French wife, Marie-Dominique—

known to everyone as Marie-Do—I'd been too bedaz-
zled to quiz her about her family. Only after the wedding
and the announcement that she was pregnant did she
reveal that they had A Secret. None of them could cook.

"But . . . that's impossible!" I protested. "Cooking
for the French is like . . ." I searched for a comparison.
". . . the English forming queues. Australians liking the
beach. Americans eating popcorn at the movies. It's . . .
genetic."

But after a few meals with my new in-laws, there was
no avoiding the truth. Academics, artists, writers, and,
in my wife's case, filmmakers, none could make a mug
of instant coffee without reading the directions on the
jar. They'd faked it with the help of Picard, the gourmet frozen-food chain, and the local *traiteurs*, who sell
ready-made dishes that need only to be reheated. But
now the secret was out. And when it became known I
could cook, they designated me family chef.

During the year, this mostly involved fielding que-
ries like "Is 'a clove of garlic' the whole bulb or just a
segment?" and "What does it mean, 'separate the eggs'?
They're already separate." Christmas dinner, however, was a different matter. Traditionally eaten in the
house of my mother-in-law, Claudine, in the village of
Richebourg, one hundred kilometers west of Paris, it

wasn't so much a meal as a ritual, with the entire clan, sometimes as many as twenty, gathered at the long table. I expressed exasperation at being saddled with this task, but secretly I relished the compliment of being asked. For someone raised in an Australian country town, to cook dinner for the cream of French society in a sixteenth-century chateau represented a fantasy fulfilled.

The family was already converging on Richebourg as Marie-Do and I got ready to leave. The trunk and backseat of our car overflowed with gifts, cooking equipment, and everything necessary to feed eighteen people—everything but the *confiture d'oignons* I was stirring on top of the stove.

"Smells good," said Marie-Do.

The apartment had filled with the tart-sweet aroma of a kilo of finely chopped red onions braised with sugar, spices, and red wine vinegar.

Christmas dinner normally began with oysters, eight dozen of which we'd ordered from Yves Papin of La Tremblade, the best in France and supplier to the president himself. But some guests didn't like oysters, so we'd made an adjustment. My brother-in-law, Jean-Marie, offered a *foie gras*, cooked and preserved at his family farm in the Dordogne. Rather than serve it with just the traditional dry rye toast, I'd made *confiture d'oignons.* Its blend of tart and sweet undercut the fat of the liver, emphasizing its luxurious creaminess.

"And I used your vinegar," I said.

The stoneware vinegar bottle was Marie-Do's sole culinary contribution to the house. Into it, she emptied the few trickles of red wine left after a dinner party. Inside, the *mère,* or mother, a gel-like colony of bacteria, transformed it into an aromatic vinegar. This bottle, with the *mère* already inside, came to Paris in 1959 with Aline, the housekeeper hired to cook for Marie-Do, her young sister, and their widowed mother. Before that, who knew? Perhaps it had provided *vinaigrette* for a salad eaten by Napoleon. Julius Caesar's cook might have used it to make that Roman favorite *In Ovis Apalis,* mixing vinegar, honey, and pine nuts as a sauce for hard-boiled eggs. As long as you kept it fed, the *mère* was immortal.

I let the confiture cool and packed it into two large jars. They exactly filled the last of the carryalls. Unlike other Christmases, which often verged on panic, this one, I'd vowed, would be properly organized.

We lowered the central heating, switched on the answering machine, and shut off our computers. We made sure that Scotty, our cat, had food and water, that his litter tray was clean, and that, if the mood took him, he could slip onto the balcony to see if snow really was as nasty as he remembered. Staring crossly through the glass at the white-blanketed terrace, he reminded me of the cat in a novel by science fiction writer Robert Heinlein. Called Petronius Arbiter, he prowls from door to door, looking for the one he remembers from August that opens onto a warm and snow-less landscape—the door into summer.

We stepped out onto the landing. Marie-Do put her key into the door.

It wouldn't turn.

She jiggled it.

The lock still refused to budge. And the key refused to come out, no matter how hard she tugged.

We went back inside and tried from the other side.

Solid.

It was a good lock. Heavy metal, with a deadbolt, and two bars that slid into slots in the floor and the door frame. In fact, it was *too* good. Because of a security feature, if we closed the door with the key inside, we wouldn't be able to open it again. We couldn't leave, but couldn't stay either.

"If you want to see God laugh," they say, "tell him your plans."

✻ · 3 · ✻

What a Man's Got to Do

To this day, someone will say "Hemingway didn't seem to have much of an education." By this, I suppose, the academic critic means Ernest hadn't taken his own formal academic drill. But as the philosophers themselves are aware, the artist kind of knowing, call it intuition if you will, could yield a different kind of knowledge, beyond rational speculation.

MORLEY CALLAGHAN, *That Summer in Paris*

You can blame Hemingway for what happened next.

Well, not *personally*. He had, after all, been dead since 1961. But his celebrations of hunting, shooting, fishing, bullfighting, and war popularized the conviction that a writer should be a person of action as well as ideas. Numerous authors, inspired by his stories of safaris, boxing matches, and battle, had been gored, shot, knocked insensible, or (not least) left with horrific hangovers trying to prove they were his equal.

I was no different. When I visualized Hemingway, I never thought of him hunched over a notepad in a rented room, working on "Hills Like White Elephants." What I remembered was Josef Karsh's stern portrait taken at the time of his 1954 Nobel Prize. The bearded face above the roll-neck sweater radiated determination. Steven Spielberg, refining his concept of the extraterrestrial E.T., clipped the forehead and nose from Karsh's image, added the eyes of poet Carl Sandburg and the mouth of Albert Einstein, and pasted them onto the photograph of a baby's face to create an archetype of patient compassion and resolve. *That* Hemingway would never be defeated by a jammed door lock.

Rummaging in our toolbox, I rehearsed how his terse prose might describe what I was about to do. *He took the pliers in his right hand. The metal was cold. They were good pliers. They had been made for a purpose, and now they were to be put to work. . .*

Watched nervously by Marie-Do *(What do women*

know of such matters? These are the things of men), I clamped the pliers onto the end of the key and pulled.

Nothing.

A twist and a yank.

Same result.

Marie-Do disappeared into the office. "I found the manufacturer's website," she called. "It says that, if the key is a duplicate, it might not have been cut correctly. It could have a 'fish hook' that stops it from being removed."

"So how *do* you remove it?"

There was a pause. "It says, 'Unscrew the whole lock and take it to a local locksmith.'"

"That's *very* useful."

"What about the locksmith on rue Dauphine. He might still be open."

"On Christmas Eve?"

Just then, the phone rang. It was my sister-in-law. "Haven't you left yet?"she inquired, sounding a little edgy. "The farmer just delivered the geese. When do you think you'll get here?"

I passed the phone to Marie-Do, who put her hand over the mouthpiece and gave me the why-are-you-still-here? look.

"I'm going, I'm going!" I said.

4

Heat

Some say the world will end in fire,
Some say in ice.
From what I've tasted of desire
I hold with those who favor fire.
ROBERT FROST, "Fire and Ice"

I half-walked, half-skated down rue de l'Odéon, avoiding the worst sheets of ice and grabbing handholds where I could. Bad enough to be locked in; worse with a broken leg.

Mentally, I forgave Hemingway. It wasn't his fault. In fact, that image of physical ease and technical competence was an illusion. In real life, Ernie was a klutz. After being blown up and wounded during World War I, the events that inspired *A Farewell to Arms*, he spent the rest of his life putting himself and others in harm's way. He barely survived some close calls running the bulls in Pamplona. In a couple of Paris boxing matches, he was knocked about by portly but nimble Canadian writer Morley Callaghan, admittedly helped by some inept timekeeping by Scott Fitzgerald—not the man any sane person would have chosen for that task.

In World War II, cruising off Cuba with the drinking pals of his "Crook Factory," he threatened the safety of everyone but the German submariners they were supposed to be hunting. The army kept him out of Europe as long as it could, but once it let him in, he played soldier all over northern France, getting into scrapes from which a friendly general had to extricate him. (Hemingway repaid him with the ambiguous compliment of making him the hero of his first postwar novel *Across the River and Into the Trees*, a notable flop.) After that, he was burned in a bushfire, smashed his knee in a 1945 car accident, and, on safari in Africa, survived two plane crashes, from which he never fully recovered.

A less life-threatening but typical accident took place in March 1928, when he lived just round the corner, on rue Ferou. After a heavy night at the Dingo Bar, he lurched to his toilet, which was equipped with an elevated cistern, and yanked the wrong chain, bringing down a skylight on his head. Archibald MacLeish applied toilet paper and drove him to the American Hospital in Neuilly, where they put nine stitches into a gash. To see him, grinning and bandaged like a veteran, posing for photos the following week in front of Shakespeare and Company, you'd think he'd fought off an armed gang with his bare hands. But, as one critic commented, employing an appropriate *corrida* metaphor, Ernest worked very close to the bull.

The end of our street, where it intersects with bou-

A bandaged Hemingway with Sylvia Beach and her staff

levard Saint-Germain, was normally the busiest in the area, but today its cafés and restaurants were shuttered and empty. In the bank at the corner, the *distributeurs*—ATMs—all flashed red. Emptied overnight, they'd remain so until next week, since the entire staff was on holiday, including the people who refilled them. In the métro, some trains would still be running but with few passengers. And nobody would be staffing the *guichets*, or ticket offices. You'd be expected to buy your tickets from the machines, feed them through the barrier, and find your own way to the platform. Soon, the métro would be like this all year round, not just at Christmas. The new lines are driverless. Computers open and close the doors and deliver us to our destination shrink-wrapped in technology.

I paused halfway across the boulevard. On an ordinary day, traffic would have mown me flat. But along the avenue, though every light was green and I could see at least five blocks in each direction, not a vehicle moved. Snow softened the buildings' outlines and misted the air. It leached out color, leaving a landscape by Whistler. To my eye, led block after block by the perspective of those six-story buildings and their meticulously aligned balconies, the boulevard embodied rationality and intellect. Let others gather at Notre

Dame, Saint Sulpice, Saint Peter's in Rome, or King's College Chapel in Cambridge to acknowledge the existence of a higher order.

My church was here.

W ithin thirty minutes, I was back home, unsuccessful.

"Closed," I said, shaking the snow off my hat.

"What now?"

At this point, I had The Idea.

To open a jar, one ran hot water over the lid, which made it expand. So obviously, if we heated the exterior of the lock cylinder, it would also expand, releasing the key.

We didn't own a blowtorch, but I had a butane torch, used for melting the sugar on crème brûlée. It roared satisfyingly as I lit it up, producing a clear blue flame.

"It won't set everything on fire?" Marie-Do asked dubiously.

"Like what? The lock housing is steel."

Turning the flame on the lock, I gripped the key with our pliers and tugged so that the moment the cylinder expanded, I could extract it.

This didn't happen.

Instead, the lock casing, which clearly *wasn't* steel, softened and tore, like uncooked pastry. Not only the key but the whole cylinder came loose, with the key still inside. It left an irregular, smoking hole.

Hemingway wrote, "A man can be destroyed, but not defeated." For the moment, I couldn't recall his thoughts about making a complete ass of oneself.

An hour later, I stood in the empty apartment, nursing a mug of coffee and staring out over the snow-covered roofs.

Marie-Do was on her way to Richebourg in the car, carrying what food we'd already prepared. The question of cooking the geese remained to be resolved.

As to the lock, it was Marie-Do who floated the option that we'd shunned so far.

"There's the card on the fridge."

We all have such cards. Headed "Useful Numbers," they materialize on doormats every few weeks. Just a list of numbers useful in an emergency: ambulance, fire service, hospitals. At first glance, they seem a generous gesture—until halfway down the list, where the nature of the services becomes less public-spirited. "Poison Hotline" is followed by "Blocked toilet?" "Water leak?" "No electricity?" and "Broken door lock?" In each case, it assures us help is at hand. But nobody *ever* rings these 24/7 plumbers, glaziers, or locksmiths, since their prices are extortionate. In France, and probably in the rest of the world, to employ these sharks was to mark yourself forever as a dumbbell—in Parisian slang, a *plouc*.

Calling the number, I half expected a recording advising us to call back in January. Instead, someone picked up on the second ring and promised to be there in an hour.

While I waited, I thought about California, where I'd lived before I came to France. Had this happened there, a neighbor would have fixed it in ten minutes. There was much I didn't miss about the United States, but one thing that I did miss was the American skill with *things*: the legendary "good old American know-how."

The foundation of this was Shop class. I never learned what constituted Shop, except that being good at it implied you were hopeless at everything else. Neither schools in Australia, where I was born and raised, nor in Britain, where I'd lived for many years, offered anything so practical. (It's conceivable that some male students at British or Australian schools learned such skills in other ways. I just *assumed* the tough kids spent recess behind the toilet block smoking and comparing the length of their penises. Maybe they were actually exchanging information on how to cut dovetails and thread pipe.) But because of Shop, most U.S. drivers carried jumper cables and spare fan belts, and a toolbox was standard in every home.

"*They* wouldn't melt a lock with a cooking torch," I said to Scotty. He mewed, and rubbed my leg. He probably only wanted food, but I took it for consolation.

5

Two Geese A-Roasting

First, catch your hare.
RECIPE FOR JUGGED HARE, *Mrs Beeton's Book*
of Household Management, 1861

H ot and stuffy, the car smelled of Four-in-One and Guerlain. The oil came from the clothes of my brother-in-law, Jean-Marie, whose car it was. He restored old motorcycles as a hobby and trailed the odor in the same way that my daughter, Louise, and Jean-Marie's daughter, Alice, bickering in the backseat, trailed perfume.

Though clearly there existed a Christmas rich in goodwill, hospitality, and tidings of comfort and joy, thanks to my problems with the front door lock we were far from it. Instead of the Rush to Beat the Rush and the

Rush itself, we'd got stuck in the Rush of Those Who Decided to Wait and Miss the Rush.

A glacier of metal crept forward in centimeters. Every few seconds, sleet sloshed across the windshield to drool like freezing spit in a gelid slush down the glass. Jean-Marie's thumb flicked the wiper control, but those few seconds showed us only the nearest cars filled with people as bored and irritated as ourselves. A man slogged past us between the cars, hands in pockets, head bowed, leaning into a storm speedily deteriorating into a blizzard. A driver whose motor had died? Someone desperate for a quiet spot to pee? Or perhaps someone not unlike myself, wandering a desolate Saint-Germain in search of a locksmith.

Was that only two hours ago?

The young locksmith had arrived within the hour and wasted no time rolling his eyes at the damage done by my torch. Before I'd finished explaining, he was unscrewing the lock.

"Is nothing," he said in approximate English. He was Spanish, maybe, or Portuguese; naturally no Frenchman would break into his Christmas. "If you close . . ." He mimed pushing the door shut. " . . . is not possible open again with this lock. So some people . . . you know . . . to get out . . ." He mimed hacking with an axe. My melting the lock didn't seem quite so stupid.

"Do you know why it wouldn't open?"

"Sure." He pulled the door open and pointed to scratches on the lock plate. "You see here, the . . ." He groped for the French word for "burglary." "I think . . . a *cambriolage*?"

Somebody had apparently tried to break in. All they'd done, however, was ruin the lock, probably by breaking off a fragment of metal inside.

*I*n the car, my mobile rang. It was Marie-Do.

"What happened?"

"He fixed it."

I didn't mention what it cost—a little over $2,000. A few times as he worked, he answered calls on his cell phone and noted down addresses. Business was good. No wonder he agreed to work over Christmas. He probably spent the rest of the year in the Bahamas.

"Where are you now?" she asked.

The snow-swept darkness gave no clue. "Somewhere on the road to Richebourg. Traffic's impossible."

"Everyone's arrived. We're just setting the table. What should we do?"

"If we want to eat before midnight, the geese should go in . . ." I looked at my watch. Six o'clock. "Now."

"I can't cook two geese!"

"It's not so hard. The others will help." Even as I said it, I recognized the absurdity of this. My in-laws could burn water. "If I have to, I can talk you through it."

Marie-Do asked uneasily, "They don't still have their . . . *stuff*?"

(In one of his comic books about the Fabulous Furry Freak Brothers, Gilbert Shelton has the dumbest brother, Fat Freddy, roast a chicken.

"This is good chicken," say his brothers. "What did you stuff it with?"

"Didn't need stuffing," says Freddy. "It wasn't empty.")

"Their stuff has been removed. Promise."

"All right," she said. "I'll get a piece of paper."

"What for?"

"The recipe."

And for the first time that day I really began to worry.

Non-cooks have a touching faith in cookbooks. They think that if you have a recipe, it's just a question of following the directions. But a cookbook is like a sex manual: if you need to consult it, you aren't doing it right.

"You don't need a recipe." I searched for a phrase that would reassure her. "They're oven-ready."

"Really?" I could feel her suspicion.

"Light the ovens, shove in the stuffing, put one goose in each oven, close the door."

"But . . ."

"Done. I promise you."

"But what about the potatoes . . . ?"

"Boil them for ten minutes, then put them in the fat under the geese. Simple."

"Are you sure we shouldn't wait . . . ?"

So that we can eat at 2 a.m.? "Absolutely not. These are foolproof. Just do as I say. Ring me if you have a problem. But you won't."

I put the phone in my pocket.

"Anybody know some good prayers?"

Of course it came out all right in the end.

We arrived at Richebourg just as the geese were ready to come out of the oven. There are better ways of supervising a dinner than on a mobile phone with a failing battery while stuck in a freeway traffic jam during a blizzard, but our success was proof that it could be done. Fortunately, the birds were so fat that they lubricated themselves and didn't suffer from being neither basted nor turned. The potatoes had roasted perfectly in the inch-deep fat that collected under them. We took the birds out, set them aside to rest before carving, and put the carrot and spinach *gratins* into the ovens to warm. At the table, plates were set out for *foie gras*, with dishes of *confiture d'oignons* and cranberry sauce, another U.S. innovation smuggled past the prejudice against foreign foods, and for the Pepin oysters Jean-Marie was busy opening. The French flair for compromise and improvisation had seen us through.

6

The Hollywood Moment

*To enter out into that silence that was the city at eight
o'clock of a misty evening in November, to put your
feet upon that buckling concrete walk, to step over
grassy seams and make your way, hands in
pockets, through the silences, that was what
Mr. Leonard Mead most dearly loved to do.*

RAY BRADBURY, "The Pedestrian"

A stuffy car at dead of night in a storm of freezing sleet had offered few opportunities for conversation. Even the radio fell silent, the signal of TSF
89.9, the all-jazz station, fraying at the limit of its range
until we wearied of the occasional scraps of Miles and
Coltrane and clicked it off. That left nothing to do but
think.

Maybe it was the frustration of our immobility, but I
thought about walking.

When I arrived in Paris, walking was the furthest thing from my mind. Two years in Los Angeles had persuaded me that going anywhere on foot wasn't just unusual but downright unnatural, even illegal.

Before that, I'd lived in England, in a real East Anglian village, East Bergholt, where one walked as a matter of course. On Sundays, my friend and I would cross the fields behind our cottage, take the track past the pond where John Constable painted *The Hay Wain*, and follow the towpath along the River Stour to the village of Dedham and a pub called The Sun. Years later, I heard this stroll described in a BBC documentary as "for three hundred years an integral part of the English experience." This was embarrassing. I should have paid more attention.

Even during the week, I walked. I'd often stroll a mile into the center of our village where one all-purpose shop doubled as market and post office. On the way back with a bag of groceries, I'd pause at one of its many pubs for a beer or cut across the fields to visit illustrator and novelist James Broom-Lynne, who never needed much excuse to be distracted. He'd designed all the covers for the twelve-volume series of novels by Anthony Powell called *A Dance to the Music of Time*, and some of Powell's amused weariness seemed to have rubbed off.

The pedestrian-free streets of Los Angeles

Occasionally, I caught a bus to the nearest large town, Colchester, or to the railway station at Manningtree and thence a train to London, where I saw my literary agent or reviewed some book or film for the BBC. I assumed I could continue more or less the same way in California.

I was wrong.

Ray Bradbury's 1951 short story "The Pedestrian" should have alerted me. It's set in a future Los Angeles where nobody walks, least of all at night. They huddle inside, behind locked doors—not out of fear so much as inertia. One man defies this custom. Passing house after house with drawn blinds, he reflects on what lies within:

"tombs, ill-lit by television light, where the people sat like the dead, the gray or multi-colored lights touching their faces, but never really touching them."

One night, a robot police car halts by him.

"What are you doing out?" it asks.
"Walking. Just walking."
"Walking where? For what?"
"Walking for air. Walking to see."

The answers condemn him. Who but a madman would walk for pleasure? He's hauled off for brainwashing at the Psychiatric Center for Research on Regressive Tendencies.

Veteran Avenue, where I lived in LA, is a long, quiet thoroughfare of low-rise apartment buildings that terminates in the campus of the University of California, Los Angeles. Next to UCLA is the square mile of stores, cinemas, churches, and markets known locally as Westwood Village. And a village was a village, whether in Los Angeles or Suffolk. If you measured such things in distance, a walk to the East Bergholt store and to Westwood were the same.

I tried it one autumn afternoon just after I arrived.

It was eerie.

Back in East Bergholt, particularly on the outskirts, houses were scattered, even isolated. A stretch of woodland might separate one from the next. No wonder the English village was such a popular setting for murder mysteries. Even so, on my walks, I'd often encounter another pedestrian, or a man trimming his hedge, and though we didn't know one another, we would exchange a nod or a "Good afternoon."

But here in Los Angeles, on a street lined with apartment buildings, presumably all occupied, I saw no one. Worse, I sensed few people had stepped on this sidewalk in a year. In doorways seldom if ever opened, supermarket catalogs and menus for Chinese restaurants had gathered in drifts, yellowed and wrinkled by sun and rain. Crabgrass insinuated itself through gaps between concrete slabs, themselves dusted with grit like sand in a pharaoh's tomb. Looking back, I saw my footprints outlined. Beyond well-tended lawns, neat signs on sticks poked up at the edge of the flower beds. In England, they would have read *Begonia acerifolia* or *Paeonia abchasica*. Here they announced: WARNING! PROTECTED BY HIGH-TECH ARMED RESPONSE.

On that first walk, I reached Westwood on foot but returned by bus, and when, shortly after, British screenwriter Troy Kennedy-Martin announced he was "leaving this bleeding town for good" and offered to sell me his car, I jumped at it. The *cinéaste* in me was intrigued by driving a vehicle formerly owned by the man who wrote one of the classic car-chase films, *The Italian Job*, and dreamed up its Mini Cooper pursuit around Turin. But mostly I craved escape from the sidewalks of LA and the paranoia of being a pedestrian.

This being Hollywood, the sale took more negotiations than a remake of *Gone With the Wind*. Finally, however, Troy, having given up his apartment, moved in with a producer friend for his last week in town. Booked on an early flight to New York, and thence to London, he still needed the car to get to the airport. So we agreed I'd take a cab to his friend's house, drive him to LAX, and keep the car afterward.

In car-owning LA, cabs are uncommon, particularly at 4:00 a.m. The driver who collected me in the velvety darkness kept the bulletproof plastic screen locked down and shot me the occasional suspicious glance in the rearview mirror. As we pulled up at the address Troy gave me, our headlights washed over an imposing stone entrance and cast-iron gates. Beyond, a gravel drive led up to the residence. Obviously he was one of the producers who made money. Or perhaps he just maintained the illusion by stretching his credit cards, which in California acquire almost infinite elasticity. As one particular billboard advertised along Sunset, with their card you could SEE A MOVIE—OR MAKE ONE.

Only the width of the drive separated the portico of the front door from the guest house, where I knew Troy was staying.

"Just wait here," I told the driver. "My friend said he'd come out."

He switched off the motor but left the lights on. The only sound was the *tick-tick-tick* of the engine block contracting in the chill.

A few seconds later, the mansion's front door opened, and Troy stepped out. He carried a toilet bag and a towel but was otherwise naked. Wisps of steam wafted from his body as, pink as a new-boiled shrimp, he tiptoed across the drive, pausing in the headlights to peer at us and give a "won't be a minute" wave.

A moment's thought would have provided the obvious explanation—finding his own shower broken, he'd used one in the house—but the driver didn't hesitate.

"Fifty bucks!" His voice cracked with panic.

I'd barely passed the bills through the safety screen before the door locks popped open. An instant later, I stood alone, watching his taillights dwindle into the dark.

This was my Hollywood Moment—that instant when a new arrival discards his former personality and reemerges as a character in the collaborative screenplay that is life in Los Angeles. Survivors swap such anecdotes, like war stories. Richard Rayner, author of *The Cloud Sketcher* and *Los Angeles Without a Map*, had just arrived from London in 1992, in the midst of the Rodney King riots, when *Granta* editor Bill Buford called.

"Get down there," he ordered. "I want a firsthand report."

Watching on TV as mobs burned and looted, Rayner demanded, "Do you want me to get *killed*?"

Buford hardly needed to think. "Not killed," he said. "*Wounded* would be good."

Standing alone in the dark of Bel Air, the smell of burning rubber mixing with the cloying sweetness of night-blooming jasmine, I felt the same synthesis of exhilaration and threat.

There is a standard phrase for moments like this, often employed with a rueful shake of the head. Mentally, I used it now.

Only in Los Angeles. . .

❋ · 7 · ❋

Hemingway's Shoes

*I would walk along the quais when I had finished work
or when I was trying to think something out. It was
easier to think if I was walking and doing something, or
seeing people doing something that they understood.*
ERNEST HEMINGWAY, *A Moveable Feast*

After the aversion therapy of Los Angeles, it took
my Paris doctor to get me back on my feet.

"Do you take any exercise at all?" she asked.

I stopped buttoning my shirt long enough to show
her my hands.

"I bite my nails a lot."

She stared, fish-eyed, over the top of her glasses. Not
great laughers, the French, and Odile, my doctor, even
less so. Interestingly, there's no French equivalent of the
phrase "bedside manner." On the list of medical priori-

ties, putting patients at ease and allaying their fears rates somewhere below selecting a fabric for the waiting-room curtains.

"For your age, your health is not bad," she conceded, "but you should play some sport."

"I detest games."

Memories crowded back of enforced sports after-noons at school, daydreaming in the outfield during interminable cricket matches or rugby games. Not day-dreaming too much, however, since, as in all forms of sport, stretches of tedium alternated with flurries of violent activity. Years later, when Michael Herr in his Vietnam memoir *Dispatches* defined these same char-acteristics as typical of war, I understood the hidden agenda of school games. The claim by the duke of Wel-lington that "the battle of Waterloo was won on the playing fields of Eton" no longer sounded nonsensical.

"Join a *club sportif* then," Odile suggested.

"Even worse!" *Club sportif* was Paris-speak for "gym." The experience of others suggested it wouldn't help. While he represented *The New Yorker* in Paris, Adam Gopnik tried one. Many exercise machines were not yet installed, and those that were didn't always work. Nor did the club provide towels—though such a service was, the receptionist explained, "envisaged": shorthand for something that might take place in the future. They did, however, present him with a welcome gift that reflected exactly the Parisian concept of health—a bag of chocolate truffles.

Carrying the battle to the enemy, I asked, "Do *you* exercise?"

Odile didn't blink. "My weight hasn't changed since college. Nor my blood pressure. But if these were my figures . . ." She tapped her computer screen with her nail. " . . . I would probably take up the marathon."

As a concession, I walked home down rue Gay-Lussac and rue Soufflot, rather than waiting for the bus.

For the first time in a while, I paid attention to the Parisians passing me. Slim and erect, showing barely a gram of excess fat, they stepped out briskly, as full of good health as they were of croissants, foie gras, fried potatoes, steak, red wine, and cheese.

How did they do it?

I reviewed the physical state of the Anglo-Saxon expatriate community. Pale, slouching, sagging, habitually out of shape—we were a sorry advertisement for the intellectual life. It was little consolation that some notable physical wrecks preceded us: Gertrude Stein, chronically obese, thanks to the cooking of her companion, Alice Toklas; Scott and Zelda Fitzgerald, invariably plastered; Henry Miller, who, if he took any exercise at all, preferred the horizontal variety, in bed with a prostitute; and shuffling James Joyce, who went everywhere by taxi, always at someone else's expense.

But then, as if to counterbalance single-handed the combined weight of this dropsical pantheon, there was Hemingway.

Back in the 1920s, when he lived on Place de la Contrescarpe, he would often have passed along this very sidewalk. It took little imagination to imagine him doing so now; I heard that light but forceful boxer's footfall as he moved to overtake me, fists clenched, arms powering, breathing deeply, perspiring but with energy undiminished by the kilometer-long walk—thinking, perhaps, of the beer and potato salad he'd enjoy for lunch at Brasserie Lipp.

Then he was past, leaving a scent of leather and fresh sweat. I watched his figure diminish, the fabric belt across the lower back of his old-fashioned tweed jacket tightening over those tensing muscles, notebook showing in his right-hand jacket pocket, his mind swimming with visions of trout in Michigan streams and the dust and blood of the bullring. I could hear him sneer, as Bill Gorton sneers to Jake Barnes in *The Sun Also Rises*: "You're an expatriate. You've lost touch with the soil.

You get precious. Fake European standards have ruined you. You drink yourself to death. You become obsessed by sex. You spend all your time talking, not working. You are an expatriate, see? You hang around cafés."

He was out of sight now, across rue Saint-Dominique, on the last downhill stretch to where the Medici Fountain spouted clear water in the sun. To his left was the green glory of the Luxembourg Gardens. Then under the colonnade of the Odéon Theatre, pausing for a few minutes to browse the booksellers' stalls. And after that, across Place de l'Odéon, and into rue de l'Odéon, descending to the little shop with the wooden sign hanging over the sidewalk, the sober face of Master Will Shaxsper. . .

Ernest, I thought, *I need your shoes.*

✻ · 8 · ✻

The Importance of Being Ernest

*Turning up from St. Germain to go home past the
bottom of the gardens to the Boulevard St. Michel one
kept Shakespeare and Company to starboard and
Adrienne Monnier's Amis des Livres to port, and felt,
as one rose with the tide toward the theatre, that one
had passed the gates of dream—though which was horn
and which was ivory, neither of those two rare friends
would ever undertake to say. Why should they?
It was enough for a confused young lawyer in a grand
and vivid time to look from one side to the other and say
to himself, as the cold came up from the river, Gide was
here on Thursday and on Monday Joyce was there.*

ARCHIBALD MACLEISH, quoted in
Paris in the Twenties by Armand Lanoux

nyone who lives in Paris ends up spending a lot of time walking. That's particularly true if you live, as we do, in the sixth of its twenty *arrondissements*, or municipalities.

The sixth, or *sixième*, is Paris's Greenwich Village or Soho. Historical and literary associations don't simply litter the streets; one has to climb over them. Between 1918 and 1935, you might, standing on the corner of rue Bonaparte and boulevard Saint-Germain, with the Deux Magots café at your back, have encountered Scott and Zelda Fitzgerald, Gertrude Stein and Alice B. Toklas, Salvador Dalí, Pablo Picasso, Djuna Barnes, Sylvia Beach, William Faulkner, Luis Buñuel, Man Ray, Josephine Baker, James Joyce, William Faulkner, e. e. cummings, William Carlos Williams, and scores more. Today, it's the most expensive district of the city. A square meter of floor space, the area covered by a single armchair, costs $15,000, but in 1922, as Hemingway wrote in *Esquire*, you could live here for a year, rent, food, and drink included, for $1,000.

Hemingway came to Paris briefly as a wounded veteran in 1918, returned as a reporter for Canadian newspapers in 1921, and lived at a number of addresses on the Left Bank for seven years, writing the novels and short stories that established his reputation. He often visited

Sylvia Beach in Shakespeare and Company

our building and ate at the same restaurants where we still eat today. We even knew a few of the same people. No wonder I was taken with the sixth.

Like everyone, I'd been seduced by *A Moveable Feast* and its picture of a bohemian paradise, inhabited by a handful of charmed foreigners whom the locals—those few who got a mention, mostly barmen and whores—held in awed respect. Reading Henry Miller's memoirs, Sylvia Beach's *Shakespeare and Company*, Morley Callaghan's *That Summer in Paris*, and *Memoirs of Montparnasse* by another Canadian, John Glassco, you could almost believe only expatriates lived there. They casually referred to the *sixième* as "the Quarter," almost as if a wall surrounded it, within which, as with Jean Gabin in the casbah of Algiers in *Pépé le Moko* and Charles Boyer in its U.S. remake, *Algiers*, normal laws didn't apply.

Most of these memoirs were written thirty years later, following a second world war. Distance lent enchantment. Looked at from postwar Europe, impoverished and split by political disputes, it was too easy for Beach, Miller, and in particular Hemingway to believe the sun had been warmer back then, the conversation wittier, the drinks more potent, the women more beautiful, the city cleaner, more honest, more innocent. "When spring came," wrote Hemingway, "even the false spring, there were no problems except where to be happiest. The only thing that could spoil a day was people, and if you could keep from making engagements, each day had no limits. People were always the limiters of happiness, except for the very few that were as good as spring itself."

The opinion of those "very few" mattered a great deal. When Scott Fitzgerald behaved badly at the Antibes home of his rich friends, Gerald and Sara Murphy, they formally barred him for a week. It was bad enough that they specified the period of exile, like grounding a teenager, but worse that Fitzgerald, when his sentence ended, slunk back into their circle.

Or take the famous incident of Hemingway "liberating" Odéon.

In July 1944, Paris, abandoned by the Germans, had not yet been claimed by the advancing Allies, who'd held back to let the French march in first with Charles de Gaulle leading the parade down the Champs-Elysées. As his entourage passed through Montparnasse, writer Leon Edel noted the damage done to its famous cafés, the Dôme, La Coupole, and the boarded-up Rotonde. "Across the gay glass fronts of another day, chairs and tables were heaped up in earthquake disorder. Down the way, at the Gare Montparnasse, Nazis in field-green were surrendering in terror or glum despair. It was strange, stranger than all fiction, to encounter at that moment, in the July twilight, scenes of a dead past."

Hemingway bypassed Montparnasse and came straight to Odéon. He hoped to salvage something of the Paris he had known before he left for the United States, Cuba, and fame. As Beach tells it,

A string of jeeps came up the street and stopped
in front of my house. I heard a deep voice calling
"Sylvia!" And everybody in the street took

up the cry of "Sylvia!" "It's Hemingway! It's
Hemingway!" cried Adrienne. I flew downstairs;
we met with a crash, he picked me up and swung
me around and kissed me while people in the street
and in the windows cheered. He was in battle dress,
grimy and bloody. A machine gun clanked on the
floor. He asked Adrienne for a piece of soap, and
she gave him her last cake.

Stirring stuff—but, alas, mostly invented. When I first moved to rue de l'Odéon, our octogenarian ground-floor neighbor, Madeleine Dechaux, still recalled that day, but not the way Beach describes it. A young woman in 1944, she watched the new arrivals from her first-floor window. Hemingway didn't shout for Sylvia. Instead—sensibly—he called up to Madeleine, asking if there were any Germans on the roof. She told him they had all fled, and by the time she walked through her apartment and out onto the stairs, the travel-stained group of mostly teenaged cameramen and journalists were crowding the lobby.

In Madame Dechaux's memory, Hemingway didn't race up the stairs. Instead, Adrienne descended to greet him while someone went to fetch Sylvia from where she was then living. She and Monnier hadn't shared the

Odéon apartment since 1937, when Adrienne began an affair with the young photographer Gisele Freund. Monnier urged Hemingway to wait there for Beach. Instead, he drew her aside, by the big green-painted radiator that still today feeds heat up the stairwell.

"Just tell me one thing," Madeleine Dechaux heard him murmur. "Sylvia didn't collaborate, did she?"

It was a revealing moment. Beneath all his bluster, the unsure adolescent in Hemingway continued to fret about what "the very few" might think.

9

The Boulevardier

*In all classes of society, one finds plenty of people
who, full of mad presumption or in a deplorable
abuse of the French language, call themselves "flaneurs"
without understanding the first elements of that art
which we do not hesitate to place next to music,
the dance, and even mathematics.*

LOUIS HUART, "Physiologie du Flaneur," 1841

In the 1860s, Emperor Napoleon III, nephew of
Napoleon Bonaparte, was terrified of revolution.
France had survived a century of internal strife, but if
one could judge from the experience of other countries,
more was imminent. As it happened, revolution never
did come. Two world wars would protect France from
civil unrest until the student-led disturbances of 1968,
still referred to with some embarrassment as *les événe-
ments*—the events. But Napoleon's generals couldn't

know that. Narrow streets and crowded tenements lent themselves to house-to-house warfare. They pestered him for broad avenues joining all the institutions of government—routes down which infantry, cavalry, and even artillery could be moved at the first murmur of trouble.

Napoleon ordered Paris rebuilt. The job went to Georges Eugene Haussmann—"Baron" Haussmann, as he liked to be styled, though he was no nobleman—who did nothing by halves. He drove his boulevards through the festering alleys and created fantasies like the Etoile—the star—where twelve of them crash together in a carousel. From its heart erupts the Arc de Triomphe, a stone colossus shouldering out of the earth.

No jutting shop front or portico was permitted to encroach on the pavement. Even the balconies that stretched the width of each new building were limited to the second and sixth floors. Most important, no building could be taller than the width of the boulevard on which it stood. With this commandment alone, he gave the emperor his military thoroughfares but guaranteed they would be sunlit from midmorning to late afternoon, with wide tree-lined sidewalks.

Comparing a map of old Paris from the time of the

Revolution with the new city created by Haussmann, in which the ancient crooked and narrow alleys had been replaced by spacious and wide boulevards, one can't help but be moved by the logic and clarity of his decisions. He made enemies, of course. He lined plenty of pockets, including his own, with the municipal contracts he negotiated. Many of the poor were made homeless. Whole districts of ancient and cheap housing were torn down, replaced by new, solid, and sanitary apartment blocks in which the former inhabitants couldn't afford to live. But he got people back onto the streets. Because of sidewalks, one could more easily go on foot to a destination rather than taking a horse or coach. Walking, formerly an unsanitary necessity, became a positive pleasure. Soon a new upwardly mobile middle class flooded in, creating a market for food, wine, clothing, and entertainment. Napoleon fired Haussmann in 1870 when the Revolution never eventuated and landowners whined about the new cost of doing business. But Haussmann lived until 1891, and saw what he had created become one of the glories of Europe.

Others who came later tried to add their signature to his. At best, they scrawled a graffito. In the 1960s, President Georges Pompidou attempted to fill the city with tower blocks. He succeeded in imposing only one—the Tour Montparnasse, Paris's lone, embarrassing skyscraper. At least François Mitterrand had the discretion to place his monument, the glass slabs of the new national library, on the edge of the city, at Tolbiac, where one needn't look at them.

André Malraux, minister of culture for both de Gaulle and Pompidou, worked with a lighter touch. Rather than meddling with the city's structure, he attended to its upkeep, reviving a law that required the exterior of every building to be cleaned at least once each decade. He told Edmond Michelet, his successor: "Je vous légue un Paris blanc"—"I bequeath you a white Paris."

If the Paris of pedestrians has heroes, they are Haussmann and Malraux. When, in the nation's ultimate accolade, Malraux's bones were transferred to the Panthéon, his simple wooden coffin lay in state for a day, guarded only by Giacometti's *L'Homme Qui Marche*—a statue, life-size, of a gangling, long-limbed man striding purposefully into the future. The god of walkers.

With wide clean streets, Parisians began to walk, and to walk for the pleasure of it. They

A typical flaneur, from
Physiologie du Flaneur, *1841*

even coined a word for this diversion. It's called *flânerie,* and someone who does it is a *flâneur.*

The boulevards remade Paris as the freeways remade Los Angeles. About LA's road system, Joan Didion wrote:

> Anyone can "drive" on the freeway, and many people with no vocation for it do, hesitating here and resisting there, losing the rhythm of the lane change, thinking about where they came from and where they are going. Actual participants think only about where they are. Actual participation requires a total surrender, a concentration so intense as to seem a kind of narcosis, a rapture-of-the-freeway. The mind goes clean. The rhythm takes over. A distortion of time occurs, the same distortion that characterizes the instant before an accident.

Walking in Paris requires the same rhythm. People who lead tours or write guides crave an itinerary, the route from A to B. The *flâneur* has no such aim. Their *promenade* exists for itself, irrespective of destination. It may involve little or no movement. One might simply remain in one place—a café, for instance—and watch what goes by. I asked writer Michael Moorcock, confined to a wheelchair at the time with a foot problem, to nominate his Most Beautiful Walk in Paris. He sent me a photo of himself seated in the middle of the Luxembourg Gardens. A square meter, correctly chosen, with all that he could see from that point, was happiness enough.

I'd been in Paris for about six years before this sense invaded me. Once our daughter Louise was old enough for kindergarten, I'd take her there, first by bus, then up rue Notre Dame des Champs—where, as it happens, Hemingway lived for a time. An avenue winding along the slope of Montparnasse, it's lined with apartment buildings and schools. We threaded through groups of slim teenagers, smoking and chattering. In other countries, boys and girls separate like oil and water, but here the sexes intermingled. They stood aside courteously as we passed, a father with his little girl by the hand: a sketch of their adult life and their future as husbands and wives.

Having delivered her to the nuns—"Au'voir, Papa
. . . Au'voir, chérie"—I often returned through the Luxembourg. One November morning the sky was that me-
tallic gray one sees in the zinc-covered roofs of Paris,
a sure sign of imminent snow, though I didn't expect,
as I entered the gardens from rue d'Assas, that it would
start at that moment. Turning my face from the wind-
driven dust of ice, stingingly cold, I passed the shuttered
puppet theater and the playground with its silent rides.
Detouring around the sandpit and the unmanned police
box, I reached the curved balustrade at the top of the
wide stone steps that led into the lower garden, directly
behind the Sénat.

All color had drained from the park, reducing it to
a photograph by Kertesz or Cartier-Bresson. Nobody
occupied the chairs that morning or sailed boats on the
pond. There was none of the gaiety and ease one associ-
ated with the gardens in summer. Yet I felt elated. As
if, like ultraviolet light, it could not penetrate glass, the
essence of Paris is lost if seen through the double glazing
of a hotel room or from the top of a tour bus. You must
be on foot, with chilled hands thrust into your pockets,
scarf wrapped round your throat, and thoughts of a hot
café crème in your imagination. It made the difference
between simply being present and being *there*.

10

The Murderer's Garden

Gardens, you are, by virtue of your curves, your abandon, your plunging gorge, and the softness of your curves, women of the mind—often stupid and wicked, but the very stuff of intoxication, of illusion.

LOUIS ARAGON, *Paris Peasant*

Walking is an excellent idea," Marie-Do said when I told her Odile's advice. "You can walk in the Luxembourg." She saw my sour look. "What's wrong with the Luxembourg?"

It all went back to those Sunday afternoons when our parents dressed us in our best outfits and dragged us to the nearest expanse of public greenery—in our case, Sydney's Centennial Park. As an adult, I came to appreciate, if not actively relish, this Victorian relic, its roads lined with palm trees, and the reedy ponds where indignant birds squabbled and squawked. And how symptomatic of Australian conservatism that some self-appointed censor had taken a hammer and chisel to the statues of Greek and Roman athletes, castrating every one, fig leaves and all. But even in infancy I recognized my natural habitat as urban. What I wanted under my feet was asphalt, not grass.

Nevertheless, next day found us walking in the Luxembourg.

"It's the park of Marie de Medici!" Marie-Do spoke with the enthusiasm you would expect from a woman who wrote her master's thesis on the Renaissance printers of Florence. She swung me around to face the block-long building of the Sénat. "This was her palace. It's an exact copy of the Palazzo Pitti in Florence."

"But the Pitti's an art gallery," I told her. "There are things to look at."

"There are things to look at here."

Over the next hour, we looked at them: fountains, flower beds, yacht pond, children's playground, puppet theater, bee farm, Botanic Association pavilion, facilities for tennis, chess, and *boules*, not to mention the original model for the Statue of Liberty. I preferred the outdoor café by the bandstand where one could read a book, enjoy an aperitif, and turn one's back on all of it.

The Luxembourg, I decided, was just Centennial Park with a French accent.

Gretchen, the mistress of meat, the poetess of pork, changed my mind.

*I*n a fit of manic hospitality, we had invited to dinner a dozen dealers in rare books visiting Paris for the annual Foire des Livres Anciens. Inspired by the season's first succulent white asparagus, I decided to serve them as a starter, steamed, with *sauce hollandaise*.

Ten minutes after the last guest arrived, I was still in the kitchen, whisking hollandaise, when a wave of perfume wafted in. The woman behind it was startling in spike heels and a hot pink dress edged in black lace. Champagne flute in hand, she peered at the lemon yellow emulsion.

"And what is this?"

The black hair she wore pinned up, and the hot pink of her dress accentuated skin a shade too slatey and shadowed to be Anglo-Saxon. Leni Riefenstahl had that skin, and Hedy Lamarr. Her accent gave a husky cadence to her voice, like *Lieder*. "Kennst du das Land wo die Zitronen blümen?" Do you know that land where the lemon trees bloom?

It says something for the impression she made that in defiance of all wisdom I stopped whisking to explain.

"Hollandaise," I said. "For the asparagus." I raised the whisk and let a ribbon dribble back into the bowl. "Not thick enough yet."

Happily, she didn't offer to help. Instead, posing herself against the edge of the table, glass in hand, she made herself available to be admired.

"In all the confusion," I said, getting back to whisking, "I didn't catch your name."

"I am Gretchen," she said. "I am the lover of . . ."

She named our most suave guest, a U.S. dealer who'd arrived with his own champagne, of a *marque* so obscure it had to be not only the best but the most expensive.

"Are you a book dealer too?"

"I was. Now I am artist."

"Painter? Sculptor? Filmmaker?"

"You would say . . . performance?" She refilled her glass from one of her lover's bottles and leaned back. Dietrich could not have been more alluring. It would not have surprised me if she began to sing "Falling in Love Again."

"My new work," she said, "is in flesh."

That was enough to stop me whisking again.

"Flesh?"

"Well, skin, at least. In Berlin . . ."

It was a hell of a story.

A few years before, her husband had abandoned her. Choosing to express her rage in meat, she planned a life-size effigy in raw pork. The plan was to dress it in one of his suits, take it into the country, set two pit bulls onto it, and, while filming it, watch them tear it apart.

"And you *did* this?"

"Almost. But *Schweinefleisch*, you know, begins to smell, and is . . . not nice. I completed only the head . . ." She paused, sniffing. "Something is burning?"

Something was burning. It was me. Mesmerized by her story, I'd backed into the gas flame and set my shirt on fire.

She rang the next day. "Hallo, hier ist Gretchen. Ist alles OK?"

"It was only a shirt," I said. "The flames never touched me."

"You are me for coffee joining, *ja*?"

I found her at that same outdoor café of the Luxembourg.

"I thought you'd suggest the Flore. Or at least Deux Magots."

"Oh, no! So . . . *gutbürgerlich* . . . how do you say— middle class?"

"And this isn't?"

She looked around at the green-painted metal chairs clustered in the shade of the huge plane trees.

"Oh, no. You don't feel . . . something?"

"Like what?"

"From the war, perhaps?" She nodded toward the Sénat. "This was Luftwaffe headquarters, I think."

She was right. The Nazi high command, sons of schoolmasters and shopkeepers, greedily seized the castles of countries they conquered. As the headwaiter in *Casablanca* says of seating Conrad Veidt's Major Strasser, "I have already given him the best, knowing he is German and would take it anyway." In Paris, the Gestapo occupied the Lutetia, the best hotel on the Left Bank, while the army grabbed the Crillon, overlooking the Place de la Concorde. Not to be outdone, Hugo Sperrle of the Luftwaffe snagged the Luxembourg Palace, where his boss, Hermann Goering, Reichsmarschall des Grossdeutschen Reiches, visited him frequently. Of Sperrle, Albert Speer observed dryly, "the Field Marshal's craving for luxury and public display ran a close second to that of his superior. He was also his match in corpulence."

Gretchen was right. Thinking of these paths strolled by jackbooted men plotting conquest did cast a shadow. At the side entrance of the Sénat, a young policewoman stood guard in a Perspex sentry box, pistol holstered at her belt. Why had I never noticed her before?

"And also, there was Landru," Gretchen said.

About Henri Désiré Landru, I knew. Between 1914 and 1918 he murdered ten women for their money. When the son of one victim became suspicious, he killed him also. And his preferred location for assignations was the Luxembourg.

An advertisement in *France Matin* baited the trap. "Widower with two children, aged 43, with comfortable income, serious and moving in good society, desires to meet widow with a view to matrimony." The details were mostly true. Landru sold used furniture, with a little swindling on the side. In his film *Monsieur Verdoux*, Chaplin's Landru-like killer is suave, even playful—a seducer. But no middle-aged war widow wanted that. They looked for someone solid, reliable—qualities writ large in Landru. He was short and billiard-ball bald, with thick eyebrows and a bushy beard of deep mahogany red that gave him a commanding air. He embodied what his victims craved: a serious man. And when he invited his prospects home, he never offered

Mass murderer Henri Désiré Landru

them anything more provocative than a glass of Madeira and a biscuit. *Such a gentleman. So correct.*

He dressed the part, too, down to a discreet ribbon on his lapel, supposedly a decoration from the Ministry of Education. Louis Aragon was so impressed he wrote, "What a pity that the court does not issue a programme in which one could print in italics: 'At court and in town, Monsieur LANDRU is outfitted by THE FASHIONABLE TAILOR.'" Jean Cocteau found his murders almost chic. "The ordinary lover disposes of his memories by putting them on the fire: letters, flowers, gloves, locks of hair. Isn't it simpler to set fire to the lady herself?"

"It seems so . . . ordinary," I said, looking around at the little cluster of chairs and tables, the green-painted kiosk, the waiter lounging in the shade.

"But it is perfect!"

I began to see it with her eyes: Landru sipping an *eau à la menthe*, leafing through *Paris Matin*, patient, waiting—while his prey paused at the gate to tidy her hair or loitered at a distance among the trees, snatching a glimpse before taking the plunge.

And where better to allay suspicion than the Luxembourg? No out-of-the-way hotels or suburban cafés, but a park, with strolling couples, nurses with baby carriages, a brass band playing, and an old woman collecting payment for the use of the chairs.

His methods, too, were conventional, even boring. Always the same advertisement, the same kind of woman, the same promise of marriage. The opening of a joint bank account into which his new fiancée deposited her savings as the traditional *dot*, or dowry, that all French brides brought to a marriage. Then, an invitation to spend the weekend at his country house in Gambais, sixty miles west of Paris. On Monday, he returned alone, emptied the bank account, removed anything of value from the house, including her furniture, which he transferred to his warehouse, and reinserted his advertisement in *Paris Matin*.

A suspicious friend alerted the police, but Landru denied everything. Where was the evidence? And indeed no body ever came to light. Neighbors at Gambais talked of Landru's kitchen stove burning late some nights, and oily smoke streaming over the fields. But sieving the ashes produced no bones—only metal buttons and catches of the kind used in women's corsets.

In the end, Landru's frugality betrayed him. He bought return tickets to Gambais for himself, but only singles for his victims. After all, they weren't coming back. He could bluster his way out of most accusations, but that detail damned him. In 1922, at Versailles, the guillotine clipped his ticket.

The house in Gambais still stands, respectable and discreet behind its well-clipped hedge and surrounded by the same flat fields across which black smoke once streamed all night long. As it happened, Richebourg was only a few kilometers away, so I occasionally passed it. Driving by, I wondered, what, for a man like that, would have been the most beautiful walk? Was it the stealthy strangler's approach to the unsuspecting widow? Or did even a murderer, strolling toward the Luxembourg and his next assignation, take a moment to enjoy the day, smile at a child, and share Louis Aragon's vision of the garden as a woman, and this garden in particular as his own, to ravish and murder?

11

Going Walkabout

Australia is an outdoor country. People only go inside to
use the toilet. And that's only a recent development.
BARRY HUMPHRIES

As if living in Los Angeles was not enough to turn me against walking, I'd been raised in rural Australia, where distances discourage the man on foot.

Well, they discouraged *me*.

Distance was only one reason to stay off the ground. Australia harbors the world's largest population of lethal animals, insects, and plants. Tiger sharks, bull ants, saltwater crocodiles, venomous snakes, jellyfish, killer wasps, vampire bats, fruits that poison, thorns that spike, vines that trip, flowers that give a rash . . . everything, it seems, is out to get you. As kids, we were warned to avoid long grass, where snakes slithered, so poisonous that one bite killed not only you, your dog, and the little sister whose hand you held but probably also the woman driving the school bus.

Lurking in slanting earth tunnels disguised with a cunning lid, trapdoor or funnel web spiders waited to launch themselves up the leg of your trousers. Old bush hands wore "bowyangs"—loops of string, just below the knee. But bowyangs wouldn't help with the redback spider, *Latrodectus hasselti*: a deadly pea-sized spider with a dashing red flash across its mostly black back. Our house, being on the outskirts of town, had only recently acquired a sewer. The lavatory was still entered from outside, a vestige of the old days when the "dunny man" visited a couple of times a week to collect the can. Redbacks often make their homes under the wooden seats of such outdoor facilities. As Clive James remarked, anyone bitten in those circumstances had only five minutes to live and an urgent problem about where to tie the tourniquet.

Not every Australian shared my prejudice against the outdoors. The aboriginal people who still live in tribal conditions, away from big cities, routinely "go walkabout," setting off into the desert, living off what they can harvest or hunt, and communing in some little-understood way with the land, which for them is the basis of their religion. Among white men, hobos, called "swagmen," trudged all over the outback, carrying their belongings in a blanket roll, or "bluey." (In local slang, this way of life was known as "humping the bluey," which caused some hilarity among Americans.) The hero of Australia's national song, "Waltzing Matilda," is a "jolly swagman" who camps where he pleases, in his

Australian swagman "humping the bluey"

case by a small lake, or billabong. He dines off "a jolly jumbuck" (a stolen sheep), is caught by the police, and drowns himself. Not everyone's concept of a cultural ideal, perhaps, but Australians love an outlaw.

Occasionally a swaggie stopped by our back door for a handout. Since we lived on the edge of town, with a rutted red clay stock trail running past our back gate, we saw more of them than other householders. Stepping off the track, they'd remove their battered felt hats, and ask politely, "Missus, could you let us have a bit of flour?"

While my mother filled a paper bag, we kids stared with fascination through the screen door.

Once, there were two men, one an aboriginal—the first I'd met. The aboriginal wore a faded blue shirt, corduroy trousers worn smooth at the knees, and nothing on his feet. Even then he looked overdressed. His friend's once-smart tweed suit was worn and patched, his cotton vest stained under the arms with concentric rings of sweat. Above all, his boots, dusty and so scuffed and scratched that one could no longer tell the leather's original color, spoke of hundreds, even thousands, of miles on the track.

Even as a child, the mechanisms of cooking interested me. "What do you make with the flour?" I asked.

The white man looked down without expression.

"Damper," he said at last.

He had an accent—guttural, European. Was he one of the emigrants forced out of Europe by the war? The group dismissed by my father as "reffos," but later rebranded by the government as "New Australians"?

I knew damper; a kind of bread, like a scone, made with flour, salt, water, and a pinch of baking soda.

"How?" By way of explaining my inquisitiveness, I added, "My dad's a pastry cook."

"We mix it up," he said after a long pause, "and bake it in the ashes."

Speaking took effort. In the isolation of the track, language shrivels for lack of use. This was probably as long a conversation as he'd had in weeks.

My mother returned. She lifted the latch and, maintaining a firm grip on the handle inside the door, passed out the paper bags of flour and salt.

"I put a bit of baking powder in, too. It's in with the flour."

"Thanks, missus." He slipped the bags into pockets stretched out of shape with long use to carry things for which they'd never been intended.

"But *how?*" I pressed. My eyes, sweeping over the things they carried—the rolled bluey and a battered billy can with a wire handle, blackened from boiling tea over an open fire—I saw no pots, no pans for mixing or baking. How did they combine the ingredients and knead them into dough, as I'd watched my father do a thousand times in the bake house?

"Don't bother the gentlemen," my mother said.

"No, it's all right, missus," said the man. "Clever kid."

He squatted so that our eyes were level. I smelled the not unpleasant odor of tobacco on his breath. Talking through the metal mesh recalled the confessional, the sense of privileged communication.

"How we make it, son," he said. "Jacky here . . ." He tilted his head toward his friend. " . . . takes off his shirt and lies down, and I mix the damper on his back." Then he winked.

Standing up, he tipped his hat. "Thanks again, missus. God bless."

They walked down the path to the back gate and stepped out onto the red dust track leading out of town. In all this time, the black man hadn't said a word or even acknowledged our existence. As they closed the back gate, I expected them to laugh, but if they did, I never heard it. I hope he knew I got the joke.

12

The Music of Walking

I am but mad north-north-west: when the wind is
southerly I know a hawk from a handsaw.
WILLIAM SHAKESPEARE, *Hamlet*

The swaggie was an icon of my childhood, an archetype who represented an Australian trait: in his case the urge to wander. Close behind in the ranks of national types came the military veteran, the Digger, followed by the humorless moralist, or wowser, represented by those people who gelded the statues in Centennial Park.

To these, we added another, more disreputable figure: the ratbag.

A ratbag has been defined as "a troublemaker or someone causing havoc." This misses the element of manic excess that makes him more treasured than deplored. For Australians, he's proof that regulations made for the convenience of the many do not necessarily apply to the dissident few.

I owed my first trip away from Australia to a classic ratbag. A few Europeans "go native" when they encounter Australia's limitless horizons, but I'd never seen the process up close until Ian, a young English academic friend, started acting oddly. With his wife, I watched in astonishment as he announced to startled colleagues that he was no longer a professor but instead the university's resident wizard, a modern Lord of Misrule like those appointed at medieval festivals to make mischief and mock the sacred. At commencement, instead of joining the other academics solemnly precessing in academic robes, he turned up in a striped neck-to-knee Edwardian swimsuit and jumped into a vat of green Jell-O. After this and other excesses, his wife decided to return to Europe without him. I went with her.

In 1987, British writer Bruce Chatwin published a book about walking in Australia. Called *The Songlines*, it was an instant critical and financial success.

Chatwin had that far-seeing thousand-yard stare I remembered from Ian, as well as the capacity to speak for hours, in flawlessly syntactical sentences, of matters about which he knew nothing at all. He had impeccable credentials as a pedestrian. He'd crossed Patagonia and written a book about it. Not a very accurate one, but an exhilarating read. He was also a tireless, mesmeric, and charming self-promoter who, socially, sexually, and intellectually, shared many characteristics with Lawrence of Arabia. Both were closet homosexuals with itchy feet and a casual way with the truth. For years, Lawrence maintained he'd been flogged and sodomized by a Turkish official during one of his clandestine expeditions in Arab dress. This was almost certainly a pornographic fantasy. Chatwin, equally fanciful, denied that his fatal disease was AIDS, contracted from one of his sexual partners, among them Rudolf Nureyev. Instead, he claimed to be suffering from an exotic fungal infection carried by spores in a Tibetan cave.

Chatwin and Lawrence wrote with a flourish of the world's emptiest places, generally with an enthusiasm the locals didn't always share. In Robert Bolt's screenplay for *Lawrence of Arabia*, Feisal, king of the Arabs whose warring tribes Lawrence unites as an army, is bewildered by his motives. "I think you are another of these desert-loving English," he says. "Doughty, Stanhope. Gordon of Khartoum. No Arab loves the desert.

We love water and green trees. There is nothing in the desert—and no man needs *nothing*."

But Lawrence thrived on nothing. So did Chatwin. And if there was nothing in the nothing to write about, he made something up. In the case of Australia, it was a theory about walking. Aboriginals "going walkabout" didn't, he claimed, do so randomly. Rather, they followed directions contained in songs learned from the tribal elders. These described a "labyrinth of invisible pathways which meander all over Australia and are known to Europeans as 'Dreaming-tracks' or 'Song-lines.'"

In the book, this is explained to Chatwin by a European emigrant he calls Arkady.

"Regardless of the words, it seems the melodic contour of the song described the nature of the land over which the song passes. So, if the Lizard Man were dragging his heels across the salt-pans of Lake Eyre, you could expect a succession of long flats, like Chopin's 'Funeral March.' If he were skipping up and down the MacDonnel escarpments, you'd have a series of arpeggios and glissandos, like Liszt's 'Hungarian Rhapsodies.'"

"So a musical phrase is a map reference?"

"Music is a memory bank for finding one's way about the world."

This was vintage ratbaggery, of the sort spoofed by Steven Spielberg in *Raiders of the Lost Ark*, where Belloq, the French archaeologist, calls the ark of the covenant "a radio for talking to God." Chatwin's informants, including Arkady, were the first to tell him he misunderstood most of what they told him and exaggerated the rest. But by then *The Songlines* was a best-seller, particularly among the "desert-loving English." At the 1987 Adelaide Festival of Arts, I ran into London literary agent Pat Kavanagh and her husband, novelist Julian Barnes. Pale-faced but resolute, they were headed for Alice Springs, and thence into the wilderness, seeking Chatwin's musical route to revelation. Hopefully, someone in "the Alice" dissuaded them and they ended their visit in the air-conditioned comfort of a four-star hotel.

13

Power Walks

Vanity made the Revolution. Liberty was just a pretext.
NAPOLEON BONAPARTE

Chatwin wasn't entirely wrong. Walks can both symbolize and communicate.

Politicians know the symbolic value of the walk. Julius Caesar, by crossing the Rubicon, hardly more than a creek, committed himself to toppling the established order. The Rubicon marked the border of Italy, and any general who crossed it at the head of his army was regarded as being in revolt against the state. Ironically, nobody now knows where the Rubicon was. It has become the *idea* of a river, like the Fleet that used to run through medieval London, the Tank Stream that served Australia's first settlers, and the Los Angeles River, now reduced to an occasional dribble down the middle of

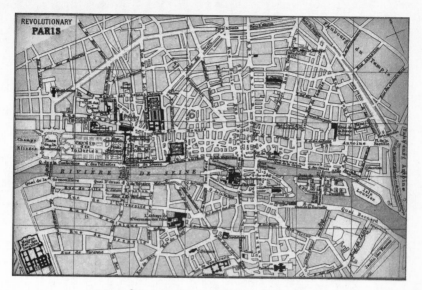

Map of Paris at the time of the 1789 Revolution

those enormous concrete culverts that deal with storm runoff and provide useful locations for movie car chases.

Like these rivers, the walk in political life exists more as a symbol than a fact. In most democratic parliaments, rival parties are ranged on opposites sides of the chamber, and changing sides is called "crossing the floor"—a short stroll, but metaphoric. In such gestures, brevity is an advantage. The Italian dictator Benito Mussolini seized power in the 1922 March on Rome, for which the Fascisti converged on the capital, scaring the

Delacroix's Liberty Leading the Revolution, *1830*

government into capitulation. But *il Duce* himself barely put foot to pavement. He let his people do the walking and only joined for the last few blocks, so as to look fresh and resolute for the press.

Since nobody walks like the French, they are the people who have raised the political walk to near perfection. Before the Revolution of 1789, the inhabitants of Paris, when they wished to protest the latest excess of the aristocracy, walked the ten miles to Versailles and shook the railings until Louis and Marie-Antoinette took notice. Today, they're less inclined to hit the bricks with such vigor and instead stage what's called a *manifestation—manif* for short—or, as we would say, a demonstration.

Manifs are a feature of life in Paris, particularly when the weather is good and the chattering classes fancy a stroll with some friends. Most bring their kids and a picnic. The level of violence is low, to the point of barely existing, since everyone understands the real impact will be made on the evening TV news. By agreement with the city authorities, *manifs* keep clear of the main thoroughfares, at least once the journalists have got their shots of a boulevard thronged with protestors. Guided into one of the more roomy squares on the outskirts, they can hold their meeting in plenty of time to get home before the kids need their tea. All that tearing up of cobbles to throw at the police is a thing of the past. If the organizers feel some violence is needed, a few energetic youngsters are fitted out with ski masks and sent at a time mutually agreed upon with the police and press to shout slogans and tear down some barricades.

Occasionally, in my first years in Paris, I watched these displays of violence in the naïve belief that they were legitimate. My lesson came in the 1990s. Out walking with Nicholas, a visitor from Australia, we found ourselves mixed up in the tail end of a *manif*, which, because it was late and the heat was oppressive, had become a little bad-tempered. On the other side of boulevard Saint-Germain, a kid heaved a café chair through a shop window. Nicholas hurried forward to look, and then simply disappeared. I searched for a while, then went home.

He turned up an hour later.

"It was incredible," he said. "One minute I'm watching this riot; the next, I'm bundled into the back of a police van and transported with a dozen other baffled Americans and Germans to the far end of the boulevard, well out of harm's way."

People are seldom injured in a *manif*, and spectators almost never, particularly if they are foreigners. Nobody wants to impair the tourist trade. Given the degree of organization and collusion between the demonstrators and the police, there's more risk of coming to harm watching a performance of *Le Malade Imaginaire* at the Comédie-Française.

The Serbian film director Dusan Makavajev, a longtime Paris resident, was the first person to alert me to how much a *manif* was really street theater.

In October 2000, watching on French TV as several hundred thousand fellow Serbs thronged the streets of

Belgrade and even drove a bulldozer into parliament, then set the building on fire, he decided he should be there.

"But you know, it is very boring. Nobody is working, so there is no electricity. We sit in the dark, cold apartment all day and watch thousands of people march by in the street, heading into the city."

Deciding he might as well walk himself, Dusan joined the next march. Almost immediately, he was buttonholed by a friend, accompanied by an Italian TV crew.

"Where's the man with the Ferrari banner?" he demanded. Apparently someone had torn down the red velvet banner with the rearing horse from the Ferrari showrooms and was leading marches with it.

Dusan hadn't seen him, but his existence did make him wonder in exactly what cause he himself was marching. He made his way to the head of the *manif,* where two men held aloft a large cloth sign stretched between two poles. He craned his neck to look.

The banner, grabbed from a supermarket, simply said SAUERKRAUT.

François Mitterrand, the president of France from 1981 to 1995, was a master of the political walk. Traditionally, the newly elected president pays a courtesy visit to the Panthéon, the massive temple with the pillared portico where the great of France lie in state. Advised by his shrewd minister of culture, Jack Lang, Mitterrand left his limo a block away and walked through the cheering mob, carrying the symbol of his party, a single red rose. The image of his lone figure mounting the steps of the Panthéon was worth a million votes.

Throughout the 1980s, every year at Pentecost, Mitterrand made another walk, up the Roche de Solutré, a monolith jutting picturesquely from the vineyards of Macon. Supposedly *résistants* met and hid out there during the war—symbolism that escaped nobody. The president led the walk, often with his black Lab, Baltique, followed by his family and members of his inner circle (including, of course, Jack Lang), plus selected journalists, who learned to watch the list of invitees for changes in the structure of power. Mitterrand himself seldom said anything. The talking was done by the walk.

For the walk that talks, however, none equals one that once saved Mitterrand's career. During his presidency, a scandal loomed when an opponent threatened to leak to *Paris Match* the details of his illegitimate daughter, who'd been brought up in the Elysée at government expense. Mitterrand got wind of this and consulted Roland

Dumas, his foreign minister and a famous schemer. At a gala that night, Dumas strolled up the steps of the presidential palace with an unprepossessing woman on his arm. Mitterrand's enemy paled. She was the madame of a brothel in the eighth *arrondissement* where he was a frequent client. The article never appeared.

14

A Proposition at Les Editeurs

What walker shall his mean ambition fix
On the false lustre of a coach and six?
O rather give me sweet content on foot,
Wrapped in virtue, and a good surtout.
JOHN GAY, "Trivia; or, Walking the Streets of
London"

I'd known Dorothy since I first came to France. She was one of the longtime American residents who, from behind the scenes, and largely out of love, manage its society of expatriates. Former booksellers, restaurateurs, diplomats, or civil servants on a pension, they're usually, like her, married to someone French, and have created over decades what the

French call a *réseau*—a network of old school friends, ex-lovers, distant relatives, and neighbors that keeps the nation functioning. No book in France receives less use than the telephone directory. To fix a leak, issue a writ, buy a car, or find a lover, your first stop is your *agenda*—a gold mine of relatives, friends, and remote acquaintances, among whom you are sure to find the expertise you need.

Through a good part of its twenty-year history, the Paris Literary Seminar, France's longest-running English-language event for writers, had occupied Dorothy's time. For one week every summer, fifty people from around the world converged on Paris to take classes with authors and poets and absorb the ambiance that inspired Stein, Baldwin, Hemingway, Faulkner, and Joyce.

The latest seminar had just begun, but Dorothy insisted on seeing me immediately at our preferred local hangout, Les Editeurs. A large, bright, and open café at the foot of my street, it has conferred on our intersection a little of the glamour once monopolized by the Deux Magots, Flore, and Brasserie Lipp, that clustered around the intersection of boulevard Saint-Germain and rue de Rennes, five blocks farther west. One U.S. journalist, seduced by its book-lined walls, red leather armchairs, and the atmosphere of a London gentlemen's club—or rather how the French imagine a London gentlemen's club might look—called Les Editeurs "a real Parisian café." I didn't have the heart to tell him it was only three years old. Before that, it had been Le Chope d'Alsace, a *real* Parisian café, at least of a certain sort: dark as a cave, even at midday, smelling of cheap wine and Gauloise cigarettes, with a carpet that clung stickily to the soles of your shoes.

Dorothy bustled in, administered the obligatory air kisses, one on each cheek, sat down, and, beginning with a bulging Filofax, proceeded to colonize the table with folders, brochures, and schedules.

"How's it going?" I asked.

"Fine, fine," she said absently.

It was a meaningless question. The seminar always went well. The concept was as adaptable as the hamburger, functional as Kleenex, simple as a shovel.

The real question was: *Why* did it work so well?

"It makes no sense," I protested when she first explained it to me. "Fifty people, mostly from the United States, pay thousands of dollars to spend a week in France, taking courses in writing?"

"Yes."

"And teachers—many of them from the United States as well—are paid to come here and teach them?"

"Correct."

"Then why don't these people save their money and get together in, I don't know, Atlantic City?"

My naiveté made her smile.

"John, it's *Paris*!"

She was too polite to append "you idiot!"

But she would have been justified in doing so. I'd ignored the oldest rule of marketing—sell the sizzle, not the steak.

Berliners are adamant that something called *Berlinerluft*—Berlin Air—seeps up from swamps under the city and has the power to inspire creativity. Angelenos will tell you there is *for sure* something in Californian sunshine that confers on movies made there a special gleam. And anybody who loves clothes will insist that nothing equals the cut of a suit made by the tailors of London's Savile Row. So a writer might think that Paris, which had stimulated so many literary figures in the past, could do the same for them. Our capacity for self-delusion appears almost infinite. Cannibals believed that if you ate part of your enemy, you acquired his courage and skill. We still believe some grains of fairy dust settle in the wake of the mighty. A Hollywood producer, walking along the beach at Malibu, saw Steven Spielberg sitting on the sand, staring at the sunset. He watched from a distance and, when Spielberg got up, slipped into the hollow left behind. Well, who's to say?

I waited for Dorothy to order a *café crème* and explain why she had summoned me. An invitation in the very middle of seminar week could only foreshadow a favor. To Dorothy, my role was twofold: as a friend and colleague, but also as part of her *réseau*.

"Doing anything this afternoon?"

Ah!

"Nothing in particular. Why?"

"You know we hold these literary walks . . ."

Nobody in the seminar cared to study every minute. Two hours a day was the limit; after that, attention wandered. For the rest of the time, they wanted to enjoy Paris—albeit while doing something literary. To accommodate them, the seminar devoted afternoons and evenings to optional extras—readings, art shows, and literary walks.

"Who's doing the walks this year?"

"It was hard to find somebody good, but we finally got . . ." And she named a moderately well known American academic: call him Andrew.

"Doesn't he teach at Harvard or someplace?"

"Stanford. But he's in Paris on a sabbatical."

"You lucked out then."

"That's what I thought."

"Why? Is there a problem?"

"I'd rather not say. But do me a favor and tag along on his walk this afternoon. I'd be interested in your opinion."

✳ · 15 · ✳

The Freedom of the City

*The traces of American expatriates, refugees, heroes
and rascals are discoverable throughout this city.*
WALTER J. P. CURLEY,
U.S. AMBASSADOR TO FRANCE, 1989–1993

*N*ext to environmental tourism, cultural tourism is the leisure industry's major growth area. For every person who hikes across Bhutan or counts butterflies in the Brazilian rain forest, another longs to plunge into the thickets of literature, unaware that it's just as full of surprises, agreeable and otherwise, as any Amazonian jungle.

Spain, Switzerland, Italy, even countries of the old

Soviet federation—all host summer events for wannabee authors. Dorothy had shown me some of their brightly colored brochures. I'd examined them with disbelief. One in Spain taught the literature and aesthetics of bullfighting, including visits to the *corrida*, though hopefully only as a spectator. Another in Rome, devoted to "The Literature of Cuisine," was simply a pretext to eat an enormous dinner every night. The only required reading was the menu.

Others were stranger still.

" 'Enforced café sitting,' " I read. " 'The students choose one of the city's historic cafés and remain there for no less than two hours, during which they observe and record the passing scene . . .' "

"I wondered if that would work here," Dorothy mused. "We have the cafés, but the proprietors don't like you to just sit. It could cost a fortune in *café crèmes*."

"Here's a woman who teaches 'Writing as Dance.' You don't actually put anything on paper—you just learn to *move* creatively."

"I noticed that one too. But she's busy through next summer."

"And this! 'Seamus O'Finnegan, author of *Learn to Love Your Novel*, offers his workshop on advanced creative techniques.' Have you seen this? He suggests you buy a soft toy or a pillow and give it the name of your project. When work is going badly, you should cuddle it or talk to it."

"Oh, Seamus. Yes. We had him two years ago."

"You're not going to tell me anyone would pay good money for that!"

"We were turning them away, John! I'd use him again, except he's booked solid. All the best people are."

O'Finnegan's shenanigans particularly irritated me. Writing shouldn't need all this voodoo. Did Hemingway cuddle a cushion called *The Sun Also Rises*? Did Fitzgerald surreptitiously squeeze his teddy bear Gatsby? (On the other hand, Henry Miller fondling a doll called Sexus did make a certain amount of sense.)

"Okay," I said. "I'll tag along with your literary walk. Like to give me a clue about what I'm looking for?"

"I prefer you keep an open mind."

Walking back home up rue de l'Odéon, I remembered a walk I'd taken at a festival in Kuopio, Finland. It wasn't actually a walk but a work of conceptual art called *Windwalk*, created by the British artist Tim Knowles. He was obviously a fan of the 1950s French theorist Guy Debord, one of the inventors of psychogeography. Like surrealism, psychogeography meant pretty well what you were pointing to when you said it, though one brave soul defined it as "a whole toy box full of playful, inventive strategies for exploring cities. Just about anything that takes pedestrians off their predictable paths and jolts them into a new awareness of the urban landscape."

Our Finnish group met in the town square and were each handed a bicycle helmet with a small triangular sail attached. The sail swiveled as the wind took it, and each of us headed in the direction it pointed. At the first corner, an eddy of wind sent half the group in one direction, the rest in another. By the end of the morning, we'd been scattered all over town. A conventional walk had become an adventure.

I'd almost reached our building when someone at my elbow said, "Excusez-moi. Je suis . . . I mean, nous sommes . . ."

"It's okay. I speak English."

They looked just like the hundreds of other couples who passed me every week: Burberrys, sensible shoes, distracted expressions, and a much-folded map.

"We're trying to find the Luxembourg Gardens."

I pointed to the colonnaded Theatre de l'Odéon at the top of the street.

"They're on the other side."

They stared at me suspiciously, then back at their map. They'd have preferred me to be French. Then they could be sure I wasn't making it up. For all they knew, I might just be another tourist, as lost as they were.

"Try turning the map around," I suggested. Perversely, Paris street maps put north at the top, but they were walking south. Cautiously, they did so.

"You're here." I indicated rue de l'Odéon. "There's the theater. And these are the gardens."

"Right!" said the husband. "You see, honey. I told you."

The wife's self-control was admirable. Instead of kicking him in the shins, she just narrowed her eyes.

"We're looking for the outdoor café," she said. "It's supposed to be very nice."

"There are three, actually," I said. "The best one is near the bandstand. On the upper level."

The wife looked around uncertainly. "And that would be . . . ?"

"I'll show you," I said.

We walked up to Place de l'Odéon and waited for a bus to maneuver its way into the street without scraping the cars illegally parked outside the Méditerranée restaurant on the corner. By folding back the glass doors along Place de l'Odéon, the owners gave the diners incomparable access to this amusing piece of street theater, as well as the view and the warm breeze. As usual

La méditerranée

2, Place de l'Odéon - 75006 PARIS
Tél. : 01 43 26 02 30 - Fax : 01 43 26 18 44
www.la-mediterranee.com
OUVERT 7 JOURS SUR 7
VOITURIER

Jean Cocteau's drawing for the restaurant La Mediterranée

in summer, chattering groups occupied every table, and the man who managed the wooden boxes of Marennes oysters was furiously opening them by the dozen while impatient waiters lined up to fill orders. Overhead, the blue canvas marquee fluttered, agitating the words "Le Méditerranée" written in a flowing hand any Parisian would recognize instantly.

"Ever heard of Jean Cocteau?" I asked.

In 1960, Cocteau had lunched here with friends and was preparing to depart. I could imagine the camel hair coat draped over his shoulders, the soft felt hat being molded between those long white fingers, ready to be placed on that leonine head; the only sight more impressive than Cocteau entering a restaurant was that of him leaving. Before bowing him out, the management asked him to sign the *livre d'or*, the guest book. Ever flamboyant, Cocteau never just *signed* anything. Instead, he decorated an entire page with a drawing so striking that the restaurant redesigned its linen, crockery, and marquee to incorporate it.

"Wow!" said the husband softly as I pointed to part of the design woven into the burgundy carpet outside the front door. They stared at it, then looked up at the marquee. A corner of this city that otherwise would have passed unnoticed came alive. I suddenly remembered a passage from *The Great Gatsby* that I'd read a thousand times, but never would again without a twinge of recognition.

> *It was lonely for a day or so until one morning some man, more recently arrived than I, stopped me on the road.*
>
> *"How do you get to West Egg village?" he asked helplessly.*
>
> *I told him. And as I walked on I was lonely no longer. I was a guide, a pathfinder, an original settler. He had casually conferred on me the freedom of the neighborhood.*

16

The Man Who Knew Too Much

The secret of being a bore is to tell everything.

VOLTAIRE

Two mornings later, Dorothy and I met again in Les Editeurs.

"You ambushed me," I said accusingly.

"Well, a little. Sorry." She didn't look contrite.

For the ten of us who assembled on rue de Rennes for the literary walk, the biggest surprise was the youth of our guide. About forty, blond, tanned, and soft-spoken, Andrew could have passed for Robert Redford's nephew. A couple of women in the group regarded him with not entirely academic interest, while the older ones wondered if they could keep up with someone so fit.

They needn't have worried.

At Deux Magots, Andrew positioned himself with his back to the café, facing busy boulevard Saint-Germain. Staring over our heads, he announced, "Here we are at one of the most famous cafés of Paris, Deux Magots. Established in . . ."

Literary memoirs often describe how a charismatic teacher ignited their interest in literature. "I longed for the next class when we would gather round the skirts of Miss Wilkins, hanging on every word as she read Emily Dickinson . . ." Whatever quality those educators possessed, Andrew had it in reverse. Having memorized Parisian cultural history down to the price of a *pipi* in the *toilettes* of Le Sélect in 1928, he wanted to be sure we knew every bit of it. One could feel the interest of the group drain away, as if sucked down some intellectual plughole. A few of us cast glances toward the chairs and tables set out on the sidewalk. *What if we sat down, just for a minute, and ordered a coffee, or even a glass of champagne . . . ?*

"I wasn't sure," Dorothy said. "But I'd heard things. People said he was a bit . . . dry."

Dry? Andrew was more than dry. He was parched. Desiccated.

He spared us nothing. History. Statistics. Quotations. Dates. And more statistics after that. Then he produced his latest book and read—or rather droned— a couple of pages. The desire with which some had looked on him gave way to distaste. Those who'd feared physical exhaustion no longer did so. Compared to this leaden progress, a walk to the mailbox was as thrilling as white-water rafting. It reminded me of something the director Terry Gilliam said about working with Robert De Niro on the film *Brazil*. The actor was so meticulous that it took weeks to shoot a few brief scenes. "We were all in awe of De Niro," said Gilliam, "then we shifted round one hundred and eighty degrees and wanted to kill him."

If Andrew's soporific lectures affected me less than the others, I put it down to having survived a traditional Catholic education, administered by the sort of priests and nuns you'd expect to find in an Australian country town. Their aim wasn't to educate but rather to create a mind barren of all information, a blank page, receptive to the church's multitudinous thou-shalt-nots. Over decades of droning lessons and Sunday sermons, I'd built up a partial immunity to boredom, in the way that repeated snakebites make you resistant to venom. Faced with Andrew, however, even my energy began to

Girls on a café terrasse, *1920s*

fail. As we reached Place Saint-Sulpice and the church towers loomed over me, I feared the consequences if I stepped inside. What if I fell into a trance, was taken for dead, and woke up a week later interred in the crypt, like a character out of Edgar Allan Poe? Rather than risk it, I dropped back, slipping away around the first corner.

Over a gin and tonic on the terrace of the Café Flore, I relaxed into the ambiance of the late afternoon. If only Andrew could see Paris as I did—the way it had been in the 1920s, when the cafés' wicker chairs spilled onto the sidewalk and new arrivals from America lingered over a glass of white wine, absorbing the street life flowing by, so unlike anything they knew at home: the taxis with their hooting *klaxons*, the *boulevardiers* in tightly fitted three-piece suits, tipping their hats to the women in their cloches and silk stockings as they shared a *fine à l'eau* with a friend and wondered what the night would bring.

The love of a city, like the love of a person, often begins in the first instant of encounter. The rest is discovery and exploration. "We didn't feel out of place," wrote the Canadian writer Morley Callaghan of his first evening in Paris.

> *The corner was like a great bowl of light, little figures moving into it and fading out, and beyond was all of Paris. Paris was around us and how could it be alien in our minds and hearts even if no Frenchman ever spoke to us? What it offered to us was what it had offered to men from other countries for hundreds of years; it was a lighted place where the imagination was free.*

Though Andrew was interested in Paris, he didn't love it. Oscar Wilde scorned such people who "know the price of everything but the value of nothing." Andrew knew the facts but not what they signified. He could recite them, but he could not bring them alive. And in a guide that's fatal.

He looked ideal," Dorothy said "Good credentials, pleasant manner. . . . *Such* a disappointment." She flourished a handful of papers and started quoting from them: " 'Frankly boring' . . . 'Not what we expected' . . . 'We didn't finish.'"

"Well, you're stuck with him, it seems."

"Not necessarily." She gave me one of her pointed looks. "Anybody can be replaced."

My sluggish perceptions finally delivered her message.

"You don't mean *me*?"

"Why not?"

"I'm no guide," I protested. "I wouldn't know where to start."

"Oh, John!" she said in exasperation. "You live here, for goodness' sake. Just tell them some of your stories."

"Stories?" I said uncertainly.

"And didn't you say you were looking for a way to get some exercise?"

"Yes . . ."

"Walking is excellent exercise."

"Well . . . let me think about it."

"Think quickly," she said.

"Why? The next seminar isn't for twelve months."

Dorothy looked cross. "You don't think I'm going to put people through that again? I told Andrew this morning that we wouldn't need him for the other two walks." She snapped her Filofax closed. "The next one's tomorrow, at three."

17

The Opium Trail

*At the next peg the Queen turned again, and this time
she said, "Speak in French when you can't think
of the English for a thing—turn out your toes as
you walk—and remember who you are!"*
LEWIS CARROLL, *Alice in Wonderland*

Standing on boulevard du Montparnasse next afternoon with an empty feeling in the pit of my stomach, I watched my first tour group convene.

Just tell them some of your stories.

How easy she made it sound.

What stories?

About whom?

A musicologist friend, in a moment of weakness,
once agreed to lecture an arts group on the history of
Western music. Plunging in at Gregorian chant, he stag-

gered out of Stockhausen and serialism two hours later to be met by an accusatory stare of a lady in the front row, who hissed "You forgot Scriabin!"

In ones and twos, the members of my group straggled out the front door—two pairs of middle-aged ladies in sensible shoes, a pretty but dazed girl who appeared to be suffering from terminal jet lag, and a short, bald man with a heavy red beard. Would it be politic to mention that he was a near-lookalike for Landru? Probably not.

"Is that everyone?"

"One other lady thought she might come," said one woman, in a heavy Southern accent. She looked over her shoulder at the empty doorway. "But I guess she changed her mind."

Six, out of a possible fifty. Word of Andrew's soporific stroll had spread.

"Perhaps we'd better start . . ."

I introduced myself, then said, almost shouting over the traffic noise, "We're standing on boulevard du Montparnasse . . ."

Within a minute, I started to feel some sympathy for Andrew. Street corners are no place to explain anything more complex than the way to the nearest métro stop. And unless you have a voice trained to project, anything you say barely travels two meters before fading into the general city din.

I had an additional problem, which had only dawned on me the previous evening as I went over my possible route. The eastern end of boulevard du Montparnasse, where the seminar held its courses, lacked even one site of literary interest. Nobody of artistic significance had lived, died, or slept here. It explained why Andrew started his tour in front of Deux Magots. At least there he had something to talk about.

Half a kilometer away lay the Luxembourg Gardens, Odéon, and a plethora of significant locations. It was just a question of going there. What would Hemingway do? I made a dangerous decision and pointed toward rue Vaugirard.

"Now we need to walk."

"How far?" asked the girl with the weary look.

"Hardly any distance at all," I lied. Buying time, I asked, "Where are you from?"

Telling me about Omaha kept her alert for two blocks, but as we began the third—and still only half-way to the Luxembourg—she faltered.

At this point, providence intervened and changed my life. By chance, we'd paused by an antique shop.

"Good grief!" I said, staring in the window. "Look at that!"

The slim metal tube, richly enameled, and prominently displayed on a stand, was obviously the star item of the shop.

"An opium pipe!" I said, mostly to myself. "Do you know how *rare* they are? You almost never see them on sale. I wonder what he wants for it . . ."

With the exception of alcohol, no narcotic exercised such a potent influence over European art and culture as opium. Alfred de Musset smoked it. Lord Byron drank it as laudanum, dissolved in spiced alcohol. Opium's chemically refined forms of morphine and heroin provided a faster, more intense sensation, but artists and thinkers preferred the drug raw. It allowed them to spend an entire evening dreaming of a world transmuted into pure movement and form. To a culture that created the vinelike curlicues of art nouveau, Monet's water lilies, and Debussy's evocation in music of fountains, clouds, and the sea, it was the ideal narcotic—organic, transcendent, and ostensibly benign.

Every arcane pleasure creates a gadgetry that, for certain enthusiasts, is as satisfying as the thing itself. Like golfers with their matched Bobby Jones woods and membership of Pebble Beach or Saint Andrews, some *opiomanes* cared less about the effect of the drug than about owning the most richly decorated pipes, the correct lamp for heating the drug, the needles for holding it in the flame, and of course using only the best opium. Indochinese Yunnan was much preferred to the cruder Benares variety, English Mud, grown by the British in India and foisted on the Chinese.

"Opium had artistic significance, you know. Picasso smoked. He said the scent of opium was the least stupid smell in the world, except for that of the sea. Jean Cocteau was an addict. One of his best books is about a detox treatment at a clinic out in Saint Cloud . . ."

A silence from behind me made me turn. All six members of my group huddled, staring.

"Oh, sorry," I said. "We should get moving."

"No, no," one woman said. "It was interesting. Go on."

"About . . . opium?"

"Yes."

How to explain the significance to the French of opium? The difference in sensibilities. How the English love sun, while the French seek shade. Opium offers no thrill, no high; rather, it's a key to the space *between* sensations . . . a state that evokes that most French of all concepts, *le ʒone . . .*

"I don't understand how you smoke it," said the bearded man, peering into the window. "I mean, the pipe has no bowl."

I explained how one took a little of the opium gum, rolled it into a pill the size of a pea, toasted it over a flame until it began to bubble, then fed it through the tiny hole in the spherical smoke chamber, where it vaporized into a few puffs of cool smoke—the stuff of dreams.

"And tell me," said the most timid of the women, "Were there really . . ." Her voice dropped. " . . . opium *dens*?"

"Of course. And still are. The French call them *fumeries*. Some are actually quite luxurious."

A circle of faces leaned close.

"You see . . ." I went on.

Even though I was almost whispering now, they heard me perfectly. I was once again witness to a truth about public speaking. It wasn't how loudly you spoke but what you had to say.

" . . . opium numbs the

Girl in an opium fumerie

sense of time. Cocteau said the effect was like stepping off the train of existence. But it takes three or four pipes to get the full effect. And for that, you need . . ."

"A place to lie down," said the bearded man.

"Exactly!"

We nodded together, no longer guide and party. Conspirators.

Two days later, as I crossed rue Vaugirard in front of the Sénat, the bookseller who has his shop opposite our apartment emerged from the post office, looked over my shoulder, and said in surprise, "But what's all this?"

Straggling across the road to join me were the people who'd signed up for my second tour—all twenty-seven of them.

I shrugged. "Mes admirateurs."

"Merde alors," he said respectfully.

As they gathered around, I said, "Now, if you look over at those railings next to the main entrance to the Luxembourg Gardens, according to Philippe Soupault, sadomasochists in the 1930s used this as a pickup spot . . ."

Hemingway might not have approved, but I knew Henry Miller would.

18

Postcards from Paris

Do not go with a so-called "Guide." These "Guides"
infest the Boulevards from the rue Royale to the
Opera. They sneak up to you, want to sell
you NAUGHTY postcards, take you to
naughty cinemas, to "houses" and
"exhibitions." Walk away from them.

BRUCE REYNOLDS, *Paris with the Lid Lifted*, 1927

"Well, they loved you," Dorothy told me trium-
phantly. She waved another sheaf of report
sheets. "Just listen . . ."

"No, please!"

I shared with Hemingway an acute embarrassment
at having people say nice things to me, particularly
when I was present. When Hemingway first met Scott
Fitzgerald in the Dingo Bar on rue Delambre, he re-
coiled from the other's compliments. As he wrote in *A*

Moveable Feast, "We still went under the system, then, that praise to the face was plain disgrace."

"A couple even asked if you did this professionally," Dorothy said. "You should think about it."

To imagine myself as a tour guide meant battling an avalanche of stereotypes.

The least offensive was represented by those individuals, umbrella or flag raised, whom I saw every day leading bedraggled crocodiles of visitors up and down rue de l'Odéon. Nobody looked too pleased, least of all the guide.

Maybe it was perverse, but I felt more empathy with the less reputable but more adventurous guides—the first cousins to the caricature William Faulkner described when he lived around the corner in 1925: "a soiled man in a subway lavatory with a palm full of French postcards." Other writers were even more scathing about guides. Basil Woon, writing in 1926 in *The Paris That's Not in the Guide Books*, claimed "the worst way [to see Paris] is with one of the professional guides who infest the boulevards and offer you obscene postcards. Most of these guides are Russians or Turks; a few are German or American. Most of them are thieves, and all are potential blackmailers." (And yes, he really was called Basil Woon. In the 1920s, Paris also harbored a journalist

Naughty postcards gave Paris a bad reputation

named Wambly Bald and the translator Bravig Imbs. It's conceivable they hid out in Paris to escape the smirks their names earned back home.)

Fictional guides possess a buccaneering quality, an element of seduction and threat absent in their real-life equivalents, who are dull sticks. Are there really professionals like Richard Gere in *American Gigolo* who hire out to lonely women visitors to Los Angeles? Initially he's their chauffeur, but driving in from the airport, he asks if it's all right to remove his cap—the male equivalent of a girl suggesting she "slip into something more comfortable." After that, his duties take on a more intimate nature. Alain Delon, oddly cast as an Italian in *The Yellow Rolls Royce*, starts as a guide to gangster George C. Scott and ends up pleasuring his girlfriend Shirley MacLaine while bodyguard Art Carney turns a blind eye. And Robert Redford, picking up two American women looking for a dirty weekend in *Havana*, takes them to the porn show at the Shanghai Theatre, then back to his apartment for a giggling threesome in the dark. In each case, everyone has a wonderful time, which is surely what we hope for from a trip abroad.

Sinister guides appear seldom in movies, and even then, their menace is ambivalent—more silly than sinister. My model would be Conrad Veidt in an obscure 1943 film called *Above Suspicion*. Most people remember him as Major Strasser in *Casablanca*, asking Humphrey Bogart, "Are you one of those people who cannot imagine the Germans in their beloved Paris?" In *Above Suspicion*, he wears a soft felt hat, tweeds, and a monocle, but he appears just as menacing. Accosting Joan Crawford and Fred MacMurray in a torture museum, he displays a pair of pincers. "This elaborate piece was a fascinating device for removing fingernails," he explains. "It is still in good working order." Pointing to a metal effigy that, when hinged open, reveals a spiked interior, he explains, "Here is the Iron Maiden of Nuremberg—sometimes known as the German Statue of Liberty." When Crawford, says, a little shakily, "You don't look very much like a guide," he observes with his sharklike smile, "And perhaps you don't look much like tourists." Disappointingly, he's a good guy in disguise. I wish he'd stayed in character at least long enough to offer Joan and Fred some postcards. Undoubtedly they'd have shown something nastier than fornication.

*Y*ou're thinking about this the wrong way," said Terrance Gelenter as we sat on the terrace of Deux Magots.

All European capitals have their Gelenter, the go-to guy of the expat culture. A transplanted Brooklynite, he'd retained the style and manner of his onetime profession, selling *schmutter* in the garment district. Where his love of Paris came from nobody knew, but it was as passionate as it was unexpected. His website, Paris-Expat.com, generated just enough income to support him in a tiny fifth-floor walk-up apartment on the far side of Père Lachaise cemetery. Not that he spent much time there. When not installed on the terrace of Deux Magots, chatting up pretty tourists and exchanging Jewish jokes with the waiters, he could be found hosting a book launch, participating in a TV or radio documentary, or officiating at a restaurant opening where, after working the room, dealing out business cards by the deck and blatantly propositioning every woman under eighty, he would, if not subdued, climb onto a table and favor the crowd with an a cappella performance of "Fly Me to the Moon."

"Is there a *right* way to think about it?"

But I'd left the question too late. His attention, always focused on the sidewalk, and the women on their way to work, had been caught by a girl crossing rue Bonaparte. His bearded face took on the look of a satyr in heat. Another five seconds and he would be bolting outside, accosting her in his inexact but rapid-fire French, offering his card, suggesting that she might care to meet him in the bar of the Hotel Lutetia that evening for *un coctel*, and after that . . . well, who knew? Because, this was, after all, Paris.

I poked his ribs, hard.

"What?"

"Concentrate, will you? What's the 'right way' to be a tour guide?"

He waved toward the departing young woman. "Did you *see* that *tuchus*?"

"Yes. But explain what you mean about 'the wrong way.'"

Reluctantly, he switched back to my problem.

"Look at it this way. You're not a guide—you're a writer."

"Yes . . ."

"But a writer who, if the money's right, finds time in his busy schedule to show you around Paris as only he knows it."

"That's just playing with words. If I offer a guiding service, I'm a guide."

"You remember that scene in *Ninotchka* where Garbo arrives in Paris and the porter takes her bag?"

Of course I remembered it. She asks him, "Why do you want to carry my bags?" The porter replies, "That is my business." And she says, "That's no business.

That's social injustice." And he replies, "That depends on the tip."

(I *missed* Billy Wilder. That he'd left behind so many wonderful films only made it worse. And he deserves credit for one of the funnier telegrams ever sent to the United States from Paris. As he left Hollywood in 1962 to cross the Atlantic for the making of *Irma La Douce*, his secretary said, "All I want from Paris is some cravats from Charvet for my husband and, for me, a real French bidet." Billy agreed and promptly forgot. He even ignored her increasingly hectoring messages. Of the many demands on his time, shopping for plumbing fixtures didn't rank high. Finally he cabled: CRAVATS SHIPPED BIDET UNAVAILABLE SUGGEST HANDSTAND IN SHOWER.)

"So it's all about the money?"

"It's *always* about the money, *bubeleh*. What do most guides charge for a walk around Paris?"

"About ten euros a head."

"Then you should charge a hundred. No, better—two hundred."

"For what?"

"For a walk around Paris."

"Who'd pay that?"

"For a morning with a real Paris writer? Who lives

in the building where Hemingway and Fitzgerald and Joyce used to hang out? You'd be surprised." Warming to the idea, he said, "I'll promote it on Paris-Expat. It'll be a sensation. You watch."

I was just about to thank him when he went on. "And I'll only take fifty percent."

19

The Ground Beneath Our Feet

In Bangkok
At twelve o'clock,
They foam at the mouth and run,
But mad dogs and Englishmen
Go out in the midday sun.

NOËL COWARD, "Mad Dogs and Englishmen"

Escaping from Gelenter and the goldfish bowl of Deux Magots, I retreated to the Chai de l'Abbaye, my favorite quiet café in rue Buci. It gave me a chance to think.

There was something crazy about the idea of taking people for a walk in Paris. Parisians grow up with the *promenade*, or stroll, as a natural part of their lives.

There are no French-language guides to walking in Paris. Why give swimming lessons to fish?

But tourists are not Parisians. Very often, like survivors of an accident, they hardly know who they are, or where, or what they are doing there. On the most fundamental of levels, the cellular, crossing the Atlantic is an ordeal from which it takes the tourist a few days to recover. Watching their moony slow-motion progress, one thinks of patients under treatment and looks for the rolling metal drip stand with its bottle and tube. The French language, which incorporates the most precise vocabulary for sensual enjoyment—*connoisseur, gourmet, bouquet*—has also contributed the best terms for nonfeeling—*ennui, cafard, longueurs*.

In her novel *Foreign Relations*, Alison Lurie suggests that when we visit a foreign country, we retain full use of only two senses. "Sight is permitted—hence the term 'sight-seeing.' The sense of taste is also encouraged, and even takes on a weird, almost sexual importance: consumption of the native food and drink becomes a highly charged event; a proof that you were 'really there.'" But sound, smell, and touch are all muffled or blocked.

She's quite right. Visitors to France suffer more than most. The language, even if you have some vocabulary, is often spoken with an incomprehensible accent and an even less penetrable *argot*. Why is a nectarine called a *brugnon*? Why is the Centre Pompidou known as Le Beaubourg? How heavy is a *livre*? Signage is the worst of all. Who but a local would know that DÉFENSE D'AFFICHER—LOI DU 21 JUILLET 1889 means NO POSTERS? Or that a restaurant that "offers" something is giving it away, but you'll have to pay for anything "proposed"?

In summer, these effects intensify. On any warm day, you can see the do-not-touch rule in action in the Luxembourg. The southernmost part of the park, running up to boulevard Saint-Michel, and known as the "Little Luxembourg," consists of two identical stretches of lawn, flanked by avenues of geometrically trimmed trees. To protect the grass, use of the lawns is strictly alternated. Each summer's day, however, a few sweating back-packers, staggering off the boulevard into the shade, glimpse the two stretches of grass, one crowded with picnickers and playing children, the other empty, and throw themselves down gratefully on the unoccupied one—only to be rousted in a minute by the indignant garden police.

As it gets hotter, energy drains out of pedestrians. Their most grievous error is to walk too fast. Begin strolling with a new arrival, and within half a block you're talking to their back. Fortunately in summer they slow down until they barely seem to move. The Canadian writer Mavis Gallant, who, unfashionably, spends August in Paris when everyone else flees to the seaside or the mountains, described the effect precisely in her story "August."

> *The movement of Paris was running down. The avenues were white and dusty, full of blowing flags and papers and torn posters, and under traffic signals there were busily aimless people, sore-footed, dressed for heat, trying to decide whether or not to cross that particular street, wondering whether Paris would be better once the street was crossed. The city's minute hand had begun to lag; in August it would stop.*

In summer and winter both, walking around Paris requires recalibration—not only a new way of walking but a different way of looking.

When I walk in New York, I look up. Manhattan is its buildings—as continually startling as the cliffs of the Grand Canyon. As much as the pyramids, they speak of the possibilities of power, the belief in perfectability, the promise of a future. In London, on the other hand, I look around. Nowhere are the social dissonances more startling, the range of physical types as varied, the languages, visual and aural, more labile. London seethes with change.

But in Paris, I look down.

("And just as well," a cynic might say, "given what you're likely to step in." This is unfair. Though the number of dogs in Paris hasn't decreased, the amount of discarded doo-doo has definitely diminished. The city has discontinued the service known derisively as *le moto-crotte*, which sent young men out on motorbikes fitted with vacuum cleaners to suck up the more obnoxious evidence. One even sees dog owners scooping up

The great Paris flood of 1910

poo in plastic bags—as unimaginable a decade ago as a Frenchman ordering *un Coca* in a café.)

No, Parisians look down because the city's story is underfoot. Though asphalt covers the larger streets and boulevards, underneath you'll find the original cubical stone cobbles: large and rough-hewn for older streets, smaller and more precisely cut where the surface is new. For a while in the late nineteenth century, the city economized by putting down brick-sized wood blocks, a cruder version of the parquet common in apartments. That ended when the Seine broke its banks in 1910. As streets flooded, the blocks swelled and riverside roads erupted into an irreparable jumble.

After that, granite cubes, bedded in sand, became standard. Often arranged in fanlike patterns, they look innocuous, but only so long as nobody pries one up and throws it, as rioting students did in 1968. The sand under the blocks was an added bonus; all over Paris, a new graffito appeared: "Sous les Paves, la plage." Under the stones, there's a beach. A *flic* knocked senseless when a block hit his helmet didn't share their elation, but bruises heal, and what remains of those days is the exhilaration of remembered passion, crystallized for me by one of the anonymous posters of *soixante-huit*: the image of a wild-haired girl, coattails flying, caught in the instant of flinging a

"Beauty Is in the Streets!" 1968 poster

stone, and the defiant delight of its black block capitals—
LA BEAUTÉ EST DANS LA RUE. Beauty is in the street!

But the students illuminated an ancient truth. If, as
the *flaneurs* claimed, walking around Paris is an art,
then the city itself is the surface on which they create.
And since Paris is ancient, that surface is not blank. Artists paint over their old work or that of others, just as
medieval scholars scraped back the surface of vellum or
parchment to use it again. Such a sheet, called a palimp-
sest, bears faintly, however often it's reused, the words
of earlier hands. And we who walk in Paris write a new
history with each step. The city we leave behind will
never be quite the same again.

20

Looking for Matisse

*How oddly the light suffuses the covered arcades
which abound in Paris in the vicinity of the main
boulevards and which are rather disturbingly named
passages, as though no one had the right to linger for
more than an instant in those sunless corridors.
A glaucous gleam, seemingly filtered through deep
water, with the special quality of pale brilliance of
a leg suddenly revealed under a lifted skirt.*

LOUIS ARAGON, *Paris Peasant*

We don't know enough millionaires, but Tim is one. An easygoing Australian, he had the good sense in the 1960s to look around a sleepy beach resort on the far north coast of New South Wales and realize that with a coat of paint and a little light carpentry, those bungalows would make ideal holiday homes. Nor did he lack buyers. People from Sydney and Brisbane were drawn to the area. Some enjoyed the climate and the proximity of the ocean, where whales swung into the bay on their way north to breed. Others were attracted by the potent weed cultivated in nearby bushland. Within a decade, Tim had three offices selling and leasing real estate and could afford to spend his spare time globe-trotting.

One Saturday, his last in Paris for this trip, we were eating breakfast on the terrace.

"I was thinking," he said, "of taking something back for the wife."

I dunked the corner of my *pain chocolat* and thought about what kind of gift a millionaire's wife might like but not already have.

"Hermès scarf? Chanel handbag?"

"Got those," he said, confirming my suspicions.

We gave it more thought as I topped up our cups and admired the sheen of the roofs of Paris in the morning sun.

"She's quite interested in painting."

"Plenty of good art-book shops around," I said. "Or we could check out the one in the Musée d'Orsay. Big stock."

He nodded thoughtfully. Then he said, "Listen—can you just *buy* a Matisse?"

An odalisque by Henri Matisse

There may be more agreeable ways to spend a warm Parisian Saturday than strolling from gallery to gallery, seeking the graceful drawings and lithographs of Henri Matisse. None, however, immediately come to mind.

We began in the arcades, or *passages*, that, starting behind the Louvre, trace a crooked path almost to the foot of the *butte* of Montmartre.

Passages Vero-Dodat, Vivienne, Panoramas, Jouffroy, and Verdeau date from the first half of the nineteenth century and share a common air of antique calm. Louis Aragon called them human aquariums. I'd rather say vivariums—those glass enclosures without water where slow-blooded lizards and frogs lounge in an artificial landscape, feeling no necessity to exert themselves, content merely to observe and be observed.

Slim cast-iron columns support glass roofs through which filters a soft, golden light. It encourages a slower pace, the saunter that marks a real *flaneur*. Underfoot, marble floors, ancient and occasionally uneven, match the tiny shops, an eccentric mix of hobbyism—rare books, antique postcards and stamps, movie memorabilia, dolls—with cafés, *pâtisseries*, and here and there a discreet hotel. The parents of Luis Buñuel spent their honeymoon in one such hotel. Buñuel himself, when he came to live in Paris, sought it out and slept there, in the bed where he was conceived—just the whimsical act one would expect from the director of *Un Chien Andalou*. Half hypnotized by the light, one's mind spins fantasies. During his stay, did he visit the nearby Musée Grevin, Paris's equivalent of Madame Tussaud's? Wax effigies of Arnold Schwarzenegger, Marilyn Monroe, and home-grown celebrities like rocker Johnny Hallyday share space with *tableaux* of Napoleon brooding outside his tent during the invasion of Egypt and the family of Louis XVI awaiting the guillotine. Might they have given him the idea for *The Criminal Life of Archibaldo de la Cruz*, whose hero conceives a passion for a shop-window dummy that he eventually incinerates?

More to the point of what Tim and I were looking for, the *passages* also include a scatter of dealers in modestly priced paintings and prints.

Almost immediately, we found our first Matisse. The pen-and-ink head of a woman, it sat among dozens of mediocre sketches and watercolors in the window of a gallery near the complex of auction rooms known as the Hôtel Drouot. Despite the bold signature, I wasn't entirely convinced it was authentic. Besides, the gallery was closed, and our lady was imprisoned behind the steel grilles that barred all the windows.

I used my mobile to ring the off-hours number painted on the door.

The owner didn't sound happy. In the background, a family chattered—and was that the rattle of plates, the clink of glasses? A late breakfast or an early lunch?

"We're closed till next week," he said. "Can't your friend come back then?"

"He's leaving for Australia on Monday."

"I don't know . . . I'm down in Bourgogne . . ."

"He's a serious buyer," I coaxed. "And he particularly wants a Matisse."

On the phone, someone in the background yelled

"A table!"—the summons to eat that no French person can resist. If the dealer had been wavering, this decided him.

"Really, I can't," he said. "I have to go. Come back when I'm open." And he rang off.

Tim looked aggrieved. "Funny way to do business. Wouldn't work back home."

"There are plenty more," I said.

But there weren't—not immediately, at least. This was partly our fault. So many side passages led to interesting little *impasses* that we frequently stopped to explore. In a shop selling postcards, I found an image of the African American dancer Josephine Baker, cheekily nude but for the skirt of velvet bananas made for her by fashion designer Paul Poiret. A few doors along, the proprietor of a tiny North African café served us coffee and an almond biscuit. Squint your eyes, and we might almost be in some Moroccan souk. . .

Our search ended back on the Left Bank, in a small gallery only a few meters from the Seine. Unlike a number we'd passed, it was open and the owner was more than happy to do business.

"Matisse? Certainly!" he said. "Please, take a seat! Coffee? A *tisane*? A glass of wine?"

Armchairs appeared. An easel was set up. From

the back room, a stately assistant carried a succession of large flat boxes. Her white-gloved hands placed an etching on the easel. A woman, bare-breasted above diaphanous silk *pantalons*, lounged on an intricately patterned rug, as indifferent to her beauty as a cat. She was an *odalisque*, a harem girl, the pampered prisoner of some wealthy North African. Her impassive, dreamy face, almond-eyed, tangled in sinuous strands of hair— it could only be Matisse.

"Now *that*"—Tim rummaged through Australia's meager stock of superlatives, and selected its ultimate expression of transcendent delight—"is *all right*."

"Picasso said," remarked the gallery owner, "that when Matisse died, his *odalisques* were his bequest to us. Picasso never saw North Africa, you know—never even left Europe—but he said he didn't need to: he could experience it through the eyes of Matisse."

Nothing sells a picture like a plug from Picasso. Tim produced a credit card of a sort I'd seen only once before. My actor friend, Don Davis, who'd lucked into a continuing role in the TV series *Stargate SG-1*, once took me to lunch at Fouquet's on the Champs-Elysées. The staff, already impressed by a famous face, almost genuflected at the sight of "The Card."

"The green I know," I said to Don. "Also the gold.

I've seen the platinum gray," I said, "and, just once, a centurion black. But this one's a first."

"Plutonium," he grinned. "No limit." He tilted his head back to look at the ceiling, a gesture that encompassed the high-priced real estate above it. "I could buy the building."

The gallery owner, to his credit, accepted Tim's card without even a raised eyebrow. After a transaction that concluded with Tim the poorer by approximately the cost of a compact car, we left his *odalisque* to be wrapped and packed.

"That was fun," he said. "Let's have some lunch."

21

Fish Story

*The beer was very cold and wonderful to drink.
The* pommes à l'huile *were firm and marinated and
the olive oil delicious. I ground black pepper over the
potatoes and moistened the bread in the olive oil. After
the first heavy draft of beer I drank and ate very slowly.
When the* pommes à l'huile *were gone I ordered another
serving of* cervelas. *This was a sausage like a heavy,
wide frankfurter split in two and covered with a special
mustard sauce. I mopped up all the oil and all of the
sauce with bread and drank the beer slowly until it began
to lose its coldness and finished it and ordered a* demi.

ERNEST HEMINGWAY, on lunching at Brasserie Lipp

For lunch, we went to Brasserie Lipp. Nobody
who comes to Paris should miss Lipp.

Brasserie means "brewery," and beer used to be
brewed in the basement of the narrow building just

a few hundred meters from the church of Saint-Germain des Près. Some of that spirit persists. The floors are still wood, the decor nineteenth-century mirrors and brass, the menu based on robust stick-to-your-ribs dishes. The primary beer served is one it makes itself. Between the wars, Lipp attracted artists more interested in good, cheap food than atmosphere. Hemingway was a regular. He particularly enjoyed its boiled *cervelas* sausage, served on cold sliced potatoes, dressed with oil.

Every important restaurant has its bijou spot, the table where you can see and be seen. For Lipp, it's the glassed-in terrace, on either side of the front door, a shop window reserved for film stars and winners of the Prix Goncourt. Tim and I were exiled to the back, which, in any event, we preferred, since the noise of conversation, reverberating across the bare floor, makes it so loud that one can't talk.

With thoughts of Hemingway, I ordered his preferred meal: *cervelas* with potato salad, washed down with a *demi*—a "half"—of the house beer, served in a large-stemmed goblet holding about half a liter.

"I'll have the sardines," Tim said—understandable for someone who lives by the Indian Ocean and routinely dines off fresh fish.

A few minutes later, our waiter returned, not with our food but with its accompaniments. First, a small glass jug of dark green olive oil. He placed it next to Tim's plate, along with a dish of slivered green onions (which the French insist on calling "white onion"). With it came half a lemon, wrapped in muslin, and clenched in metal grips to aid squeezing. A few minutes later, he returned with a metal dish holding thin dry rye toast wrapped in a linen napkin.

At last, our food arrived. My sausage and potatoes were plonked down with the lack of ceremony they deserved. But Tim had clearly ordered something out of the ordinary, which deserved the appropriate presentation. Producing a plate on which lay a napkin-covered object, the waiter whipped it off to reveal—a can of sardines.

Displaying the label to a startled Tim as he would a bottle of wine, he unrolled the lid, upended the contents onto a plate, and, with a cheery "Bon appétit!," retired.

I should have noticed Tim's astonishment. He'd been expecting fresh grilled sardines—a commonplace in Australian restaurants. It never occurred to me to explain that, to the French, certain canned sardines are of such quality that they achieve vintage status. The best are caught in the spring when the fish are fattest, and are reserved for "gourmet" use. Some canners roast or sauté the fish before canning. A connoisseur described their flavor as "complex, almost a non-fish thing, very nutty, deep, and enthralling." "Label rouge" sardines are even more specialized. Guaranteed to have been landed no more than twelve hours after being caught, and arriving at the factory within four hours of landing, they are cleaned the same day, fried in sunflower oil, stored for four months before sale, and then issued with a label that lists not only the day of catch but the name of the boat that caught them. One of the main processors, Connetable, produces a "vintage" sardine that retails at $14 a can. Buyers are advised to "put down" these like wine for a few years, turning them occasionally to spread the flavor.

"What really threw me," Tim said later, "was the fact that you didn't bat an eyelash. I thought it was some sort of practical joke."

He should have realized that the French, serious at the best of times, become positively reverent when it comes to food.

Animators at the Walt Disney studios in the 1930s thought it would be amusing to make a porno cartoon of Mickey Mouse.

Walt laughed as much as everyone else—then fired

them all. Word soon got round: Rule number 1 at Disney was "Don't fuck with the mouse."

In France, the same applies to what goes in your mouth. You don't fuck with the food. Not even the unassuming sardine.

After a Matisse and a lunch at Lipp, there wasn't much hope of improving the day, so we didn't try. At four, as the waiters cleaned up the tables from lunch and began to set them for the dinner trade, Tim and I were still dawdling over our third coffee and fourth (or was it fifth?) Calvados.

Of course I should have been working. But whenever a remaining scrap of Puritanism whispers that there's something disreputable about taking pleasure in *flanerie*, I think of Catherine Deneuve.

For many years, she was our neighbor, living in a glass-walled apartment high above Place Saint-Sulpice. Occasionally we'd meet—standing in line at Poilane when Paris's best baker had only one small shop, on rue du Four, or in one of the *brocantes* we both love to haunt. I'd interviewed her a few times, once in the salon of Yves Saint Laurent, where she arrived in a blue linen suit as crisp and unwrinkled as new money.

Deneuve was twenty-five and at the height of her blond beauty when she filmed Françoise Sagan's novel

La Chamade (*Heartbeat*) in 1968. Her character, Lucile, is the pampered mistress of wealthy fortyish Charles, played by Michel Piccoli. Seeing she's attracted to a young journalist, he lets her leave him to live in his cramped apartment, gambling, sensibly, that it won't last. Having to sell her jewels and travel by bus sours Lucile from living on, as the French say, "love and fresh water," but, this being France, the real revelation comes from literature, William Faulkner's *The Wild Palms*— the story, as it happens, of a man who abandons city comfort to run off to the wilderness with his lover.

During one lunch hour, she's reading it at the counter of a café as she nibbles her *baguette jambon fromage*. One passage so strikes her that she calls for attention and, as the whole café falls silent, she reads it aloud.

It's idleness breeds all our virtues, our most bearable qualities—contemplation, equableness, laziness, letting other people alone; good digestion mental and physical: the wisdom to concentrate on fleshly pleasures—eating and evacuating and fornication and sitting in the sun—than which there is nothing better, nothing to match, nothing else in all this world but to live for the short time you are loaned breath, to be alive and know it. It is one of

what we call the prime virtues—thrift, industry,
independence—that breeds all the vices—
fanaticism, smugness, meddling, fear, and worst of
all, respectability.

The whole café breaks into spontaneous applause. We see what these wage slaves are thinking: *If only I dared...*

Lucile does dare. She abandons her lover and returns to the good life. The last shot of the film, appropriately, shows her heading back to an existence of champagne, Mozart, Saint-Tropez and Saint Laurent. And being a true Parisienne, she is, of course, striding out in confidence, defiantly in the middle of the road, and—how else, in this most wonderful city for walkers?—on foot.

22

The Great La Coupole Roundup

Try to learn to breathe deeply, really to taste food
when you eat, and when you sleep, really to sleep.
Try as much as possible to be wholly alive with all
your might, and when you laugh, laugh like hell.
And when you get angry, get good and angry. Try
to be alive. You will be dead soon enough.
ERNEST HEMINGWAY, advice to young writers

Gelenter, operating as always on the principle that if a spoonful was good, the whole bottle had to be better, allocated me an entire subsite on Paris Through Expatriate Eyes, with photographs, an interview, praise for my books, and a hard-sell ad for my services as a guide. Because the site linked to numerous travel agencies, publishers, restaurants, and airlines, my name was soon popping up whenever anyone Googled "Paris tourism."

"You took my advice," said Dorothy, next time we met for coffee. "About the tours."

"Oh . . . yes . . ."

I blushed like a vicar caught emerging from a motel with the church organist. But she dismissed my scruples.

"All sorts of people are making a fortune out of literary Paris. Why not you?"

I found out why not when Gelenter produced my first clients.

Billie Jean, Bobby Jane, and Mary Beth (or was it Mary Jane, Billie Bob, and Jeanie Beth?) all came from Amarillo, Texas. Though none wore Stetsons or high-heeled riding boots, the way they stood, heads tilted back, as if looking out from under a brim, and rocked back slightly on the heels, feeling for a support that wasn't there, told me this was their habitual attire.

"Have you been to Paris before?" I asked hopefully. If they had, it wouldn't be necessary for me to explain everything from scratch.

"Nope," one replied.

"Never," said her friend.

"First time away from the ol' U. S. of A.," added the third.

More striking than their names was their size. Had Rubens, with his taste for massive pink ladies, needed to depict the Three Graces, this trio would have served as perfect models.

"Speak any French?"

"No," said Billie Jean, or perhaps it was Bobby Jane.

"Not a word," said the second.

The third tilted her head back even farther, and stared. "You *funnin'*?"

Increasingly alarmed, I asked, "Um, is there some aspect of Paris that particularly interests you?"

"How do ya mean?"

"Well, have you read any of the writers who lived here? Scott Fitzgerald? Henry Miller? Hemingway?"

A collective frown gathered above them, like a cartoon balloon enclosing a huge question mark.

"Maybe if we just set off?" I muttered.

For the next hour, I led them through the alleys of Saint-Germain des Près, pointing out features that didn't involve literature, history, or art: 20 rue Jacob where Nathalie Clifford Barney, doyenne of Paris lesbians, held court and built her Temple to Friendship into which she lured her prettier guests. The quiet gem of

Place von Furstemberg, where five tall chestnuts cast dappled light across the golden stone façades. That day, a *Vogue* photographer was shooting, and we watched a while as the impossibly slim models, supple as lizards, lounged and posed against the belle époque street lamp.

But as we crossed rue Vaugirard into the Luxembourg Gardens, it was clear my clients were losing interest. Whatever they had hoped to discover in Paris, it was eluding them, and I was to blame.

Foolishly hoping they might have heard of Gertrude Stein, I led them into rue de Fleurus, heading for her apartment. At the intersection with rue d'Assas, inspiration struck.

There, on the opposite corner, was one of Paris's temples to overindulgence; a Notre Dame of excess. From its doors, invitingly open on this warm morning, drifted odors no sensualist could resist.

"Do any of you happen to like chocolate?" I asked.

Three hours later, the waiters at La Coupole had mostly gone home, leaving us to a pair of *stagiaires*—trainees. They did their best to remain good-humored while responding to demands for just one more pot of coffee and "a few more of those li'l bitty sugar cookie things," but it was obvious they desperately wanted us to pay *l'addition* and leave.

The café La Coupole, Montparnasse, early 1930s

My three Texas graces had no intention of doing so. After a slow start, they were at last having a wonderful time.

It began with hot chocolate at the little café next to Christian Constant's boutique in rue de Fleurus.

Constant, I explained, claimed to have rediscovered the ancient Mayan idea of adding red pepper to hot chocolate, as popularized in the novel and film *Chocolat*, in which Juliette Binoche revitalizes a village with its delicious, addictive products.

"You mean they invented it right here?"

"So he says." I pointed to the Mayan hot chocolate listed on the menu.

"Chocolate with *chili*?" She slapped the tabletop hard. "Bring it *on*!"

After that, there was no doubt which aspect of Paris interested them.

They'd never heard of Gertrude Stein but liked my story of Alice B. Toklas's recipe for hashish fudge and what happened when I whipped up a batch for a reception at the staid American Library.

We detoured to browse the open-air food market that straggled down boulevard Raspail. The merchants' habit of offering a *goutée*—a sliver of cheese or sausage on the tip of their carving knives—sent the trio into rhapsodies.

"Shee-it!" said Mary Jane. "This is like a bar lunch—and it's free!"

With food inside them, they blossomed. How could I ever have had difficulty tellling them apart? They were as different as the three bears.

"It'd be more like a bar lunch if there was sumthin' to drink," Billie Joe interjected.

"No problem!"

Within ten minutes, we were entering La Coupole.

The last of the great cafés, it opened in 1927—the first to combine café, bar, and restaurant under the same roof. The café ran along the boulevard. The main room, under the *coupole*, or cupola, was a restaurant, with the American bar to its left. And in the basement, a dance hall. At the time, old Paris hands disapproved of this "new, flaunting, German-looking café," as one put it, but the tourists flocked there.

I tried to explain its cultural importance, but only one aspect interested these ladies.

"You suppose that bar has bourbon?"

It did: three brands. They organized a taste test so that I could savor the differences. Then Jules the barman—we were all on first-name terms by then—inquired whether they had ever tried bourbon with absinthe.

"Absinthe," said Betty. "Now, ain't that poison?"

"And illegal?"

Jules's shrug implied that such things, even if true, signified nothing between old friends.

"Je propose," Jules murmured, "un Tremblement de Terre."

"An Earthquake?" I said. "What's in that exactly?"

"Oh, pas grand chose," he said. "Le gin, le bourbon, et l'absinthe—et du glaçon, évidemment."

"Evidemment. Rafraîchissant, sans doute." One could hardly have a cocktail without *glaçon*—ice.

The Earthquake lived up to its name, to the extent

that another round was needed to steady ourselves. After that, a compassionate *maître d'* led us to our table.

For the next two hours, we stampeded through the menu like the Four Horsemen of the Apocalypse. *Confit de canard, boeuf bourguignon, poulet rôti, navarin d'agneau, blanquette* . . . little went untasted, providing its primary ingredient was meat. Even classic French *tartare*—minced raw filet steak, seasoned with chives, black pepper, Worcestershire sauce and Tabasco—met with their approval.

"Just like chili," said Mary Beth, shoveling down a forkful. "Only ya don' *cook* it! I'm gonna serve this sucker first barbecue I do back home."

She was just as enthusiastic about the Belgian beer that washed it down. ("Wine's for fags and bums," she confided in a whisper loud enough to be heard at every nearby table; fortunately, none of our neighbors knew English.)

"What am I eatin' here exactly?" Mary Beth inquired about one dish. "I'm not sayin' I don't like it. I just wonder what it is."

"Sweetbreads," I said, "with walnuts."

"Ain't that *testicules*?" demanded Billie Jean from the other end of the table. Heads lifted all around, and I felt dozens of eyes.

"No, it's . . . something else," I said hurriedly. "From the neck, I think."

"Oh, shit," Billie Jean said, "don't matter to me if it's balls, brains, or assholes. I et 'em all some time or other. Cooked *and* raw."

Before I needed to think too much about Billie Jean biting into a raw bull's testicle like a Jonathan apple, she looked round the restaurant in satisfaction.

"Hell, I *love* Paris."

I saw with clarity what my Literary Seminar group had shown me and the Texas Trio had reinforced.

Visitors didn't want *their* Paris.

They wanted *mine*.

Plenty of time when they got home to read Flaubert or a history of the French Revolution. What they wanted now was to reach out and touch the living flesh—to devour and be devoured.

❋ · 23 · ❋

Liver Lover

My idea of heaven is eating pâtés
de foie gras *to the sound of trumpets.*
SYDNEY SMITH (1771–1845)

*I*t was an idyllic time to be in France. The euro was
strong, the country calm, the wine harvest satis-
factory, the sun warm. Staying out of the Iraq War
and shrugging off gibes about "cheese-eating surrender monkeys" and the sneer of General "Stormin'
Norman" Schwarzkopf that "going to war without
France was like going deer hunting without your accordion" had proved the smart move. Nationals and
expats alike gloated as the administration of George
W. Bush came unglued.

Nobody anticipated the financial crash lurking
behind the war news, but had the French done so, they

would not have behaved differently. Europe has a tradition of enjoying the failure of others—the Germans, of course, invented a word for it, schadenfreude—and, capturing this spirit, de Rochefoucauld said, more or less, "It is not enough to succeed. Your best friend must fail."

The Austrians in particular relish despair. They're masters of masochistic melancholy—characteristics I valued in the music of Mahler and Strauss and the art of Schiele and Klimt long before I first visited Vienna. On later visits, a friend at the Österreichisches Filmmuseum, the Austrian film archive, would greet me with weary cordiality, then launch into a recitation of recent disasters, political and personal.

After half an hour of misery, he'd shrug and say, "But we always have Demel." Then we'd walk across to Michaelerplatz and the great Café Demel. Dating to 1786, its crystal chandeliers and huge mirrors exuded luxury and appetite. A waitress would trundle up its multilevel pastry trolley, each glass shelf loaded with greater invitations to gorging. The prize for sheer excess went to an object shaped like a large cabbage: a shell of white chocolate, filled with whipped cream, flavored with kirsch cherry liqueur. Demel and its *Konditorei* embodied what Vienna implicitly believed—that joy

and misery are faces of the same coin. The bitter chocolate in a *Sachertorte*'s outer shell only made more piercing
the acid sweetness of the underlying raspberry glaze.

Of Vienna's artistic heroes, my favorite was Max
Reinhardt, Europe's most innovative theater producer
between the wars. In the late 1930s, as Germany eyed its
neighbors and Hitler made speeches about lebensraum,
Max continued to direct the annual Salzburg Festival,
concluding each night with a midnight supper for the
glitterati at his castle, Leopoldskron.

As the last horse-drawn carriages pulled away at two
or three in the morning, Reinhardt whispered to a few
close friends "Stay for an hour." The playwright Carl
Zuckmayer wrote: "It was somewhat like Versailles in
the days of the Bastille, only more alert, more aware,
intellectually more lucid. Once, at a late hour, I heard
Reinhardt say, almost with satisfaction, 'The nicest part
of these festival summers is that each one may be the
last.' After a pause, he added. 'You can feel the taste of
transitoriness on your tongue.'"

It takes imagination to see food from the point of
view of an oppressed people who, for generations, were
often forced to eat things that more pampered eaters find
unpalatable. Only the rich can afford to discard the en-
trails, skin, beaks, and claws of the birds they eat; the

intestines, blood, ears, and tail of the pig; the tongue and stomach of the cow. It's no coincidence that Jewish cooking is among the richest in dishes using those parts of the animal others throw away. Similarly, the dispossessed and impoverished people of the American South, both black and white, created a cuisine from the poorest cuts of pork and the bitter greens nobody else would eat.

Such dishes become emblems of national pride, reminders of a harsh heritage. If their production or consumption involves pain and even danger, then all the better. The Japanese eat fugu, a fish largely without flavor, not so much despite the fact that it contains a potentially fatal toxin but *because* it does. In Holland, at certain times of year, the new herring are so delectable that fish lovers gorge them raw, ignoring the warning that the fish can contain a deadly parasite. For the French, to smoke unfiltered cigarettes, eat cheese made from unpasteurized milk, and enjoy *foie gras* are affirmations of their culture, a tip of the hat to times when caution and compassion were luxuries they could not afford.

My own introduction to *foie gras* was, in a way, my introduction to France, and to the rigor that sustained its apparent self-indulgence. On a visit to Paris in the 1970s, when Marie-Dominique was my girlfriend and not my wife, we lunched at one of the big brasseries near the Gare du Nord, where, she suggested I might enjoy *foie gras* as a starter.

Well, try anything once. And I didn't want to appear gauche by admitting it was my first time.

The thin slices of liver, gleaming gold and beige with the slickness of fat, arrived, garnished with the *gelée* that gathers when it's cooked. A metal dish contained slices of thin dry toast folded in a napkin.

"There's no butter," I said, scanning the table.

"Why do you need butter?"

"For the toast."

"For *foie gras*, you don't butter the toast."

"Dry toast isn't very inviting," I protested. "Couldn't we ask the waiter?"

"Non!"

Her vehemence was startling. I shut up and ate my toast dry—to find, of course, that she was perfectly right. *Foie gras* is as fatty as butter and to combine the two would have been absurd. Even worse, from the French point of view, it would have transgressed the spirit of *comme il faut*—the way things should be. In doing so, it would have also, which was worse, invited the derision of the waiting staff ("Can you believe, this *plouc* of a tourist wanted butter with *foie gras*!") and thus made us look foolish. This had already happened on an earlier trip to Paris for the BBC. After a hard day of interviews, the producer and I returned to our hotel and, not realizing the French never drink cognac before dinner, ordered a reviving Courvoisier while we waited for Marie-Do, whom we were taking to dinner. As she sat down, the waiter asked superciliously, "Mademoiselle also desires a *digestif*?"

Seduction often begins with taste. There is no kiss like the first kiss with lipstick, no surprise like the first oyster or the first olive. Nobody forgets Louise Brooks in *Diary of a Lost Girl* being offered a glass of champagne in the brothel and, after some initial doubts, swallowing it, along with the lifestyle it represents. Or Giulietta Masina as the neglected wife in *Juliet of the Spirits*, accepting from a suave Spaniard a glass of sangria—an exotic concoction in those days—and being told, coaxingly, "It satisfies all thirsts, even those that are unexpressed."

The Texas trio taught me that I could best seduce newcomers to an appreciation of Paris not through the intellect but through taste.

And no taste proved more effective than that of *foie gras*.

I'd begun to structure my walks to conclude on boulevard de Montparnasse just after noon. If my clients asked me to suggest a good restaurant, I drew their attention to La Coupole. When they invited me to join them, as they often did, I was more than happy to guide them through the elaborate menu.

"Well," I'd begin, "I know what *I'm* having . . ." and point to one of the house specialties—a slice of *foie gras* and a glass of cold, sweet white wine.

"Of course, the wine should be a Sauternes," I'd confidently explain as the waiter poured the Alsatian *Gewürztraminer*, "and the *foie gras* should be goose, not duck. But this will give you the idea."

There was enormous pleasure in watching their first tentative nibble and sip, then the dawning realization that they were experiencing one of the great combinations of flavor, texture, and aroma, on a level with bacon and eggs, apples and cinnamon, Roquefort and Bordeaux. The fat of the *foie gras* was subdued by the toast, then chased by the sharpness of the wine, the fruitiness of which prepared the palate for the next bite.

I was, in effect, practicing seduction, luring them away from Big Macs and Mountain Dew. With each bite, they became less American, ready to enjoy the pleasures of France.

In *Ninotchka*, the three renegade Soviet commissars, Buljanof, Iranoff, and Kopalski, defect to the West and open a restaurant. Their former protector, Ninotchka, played by Greta Garbo, is aghast. "You mean you are deserting Russia?" she asks. "Oh, Ninotchka," Kopalski replies. "Don't call it desertion. Our little restaurant, that is our Russia, the Russia of borscht, the Russia of beef Stroganoff, of blinis and sour cream . . ." "The Russia of piroshky, people will eat and love it," says Iranof. "And we are not only serving good food, we are serving our country, we are making friends," says Buljanof.

Well, I was serving my country too—or at least the country that had given me a home and brought me to an appreciation of so much that I now valued. Food is the international language. I might speak it with an Australian accent, but I was making myself understood.

Paris When it Sizzled

*Why are we so full of restraint? Why do we not give in
all directions? Is it fear of losing ourselves? Until we do
lose ourselves there is no hope of finding ourselves.*
HENRY MILLER, *The World of Sex*

Thanks to Gelenter, and helped by word of mouth,
I soon had more tour clients than I could handle.
Each Monday morning, and occasionally on other days
as well, I'd leave home at 9:40 and stroll along boulevard Saint-Germain to Deux Magots, where my guests
of the day were waiting.

My afternoon with Andrew had shown the error of
telling too much. With each tour, I omitted a little more
information and covered a little less ground. Nobody
remembered a statistic, but an anecdote could stick like
a burr, and an image imprint itself on the imagination.

Combing the best that had been written about Paris or depicted by its artists, I compiled a portfolio small enough to be carried on every walk.

How best to evoke the Paris that Hemingway and others like him first encountered after World War I: buildings black with centuries of grime, gutters running with waste water and food slops on which goats, dogs, and chickens fed? In words, nothing bettered George Orwell's sour descriptions in *Down and Out in Paris and London*, written when he worked as a *plongeur*, a dishwasher in a Right Bank hotel, but lived in a Left Bank slum.

> *The walls were as thin as matchwood, and to hide the cracks they had been covered with layer after layer of pink paper, which had come loose and housed innumerable bugs. Near the ceiling long lines of bugs marched all day like columns of soldiers, and at night came down ravenously hungry, so that one had to get up every few hours and kill them in hecatombs.*

But a photograph of such a room by Brassaï or Eli Lotar, or a street scene by Atget, told the story even better.

What did Le Dôme look like when Henry Miller loitered there, sipping *pastis*, watching the saucers pile up, and scanning the crowd for some acquaintance who'd pay his tab? Well, here's a picture as it was when the untidy, unwashed Miller frequented it. And one of the Rotonde, too—not the expensive and smart café of today, but the noisy hangout of wannabee artists, hookers, and miscellaneous mysteries that Miller and Hemingway knew.

Sometimes I'd bring along the kind of saucer served under the aperitifs and cafés, each one printed with the price of the drink, so that even the most forgetful waiter needed simply to tote up the pile at the drinker's elbow. At other times, I'd produce an absinthe spoon and show

The Rotonde café, Montparnasse, 1920s

how one balanced it across the glass, placed a cube of sugar in the middle, then trickled ice water through it into the opalescent emerald fluid, the "green fairy" that supposedly drove drinkers mad but, as recompense, endowed them with vivid dreams.

Most of my clients needed little to stir the imagination. They would not have come to Paris if they were not already halfway convinced. Jean-Paul Sartre, in his sharpest insight, realized that "existence precedes essence," that we act first, then find a philosophy to explain our actions. There are no "natural laws"—only those we make for ourselves. Every week, I'd see Sartre vindicated as some Ohio schoolteacher or advertising executive from Santa Barbara ran a hand over the counter of a café on rue Jacob while I explained it was at *this very bar* that Fitzgerald and Hemingway stood when a tearful Scott confessed that "Zelda said that the way I was built I could never make a woman happy. . . . She said it was a matter of measurements."

"And if you wish," I pointed to narrow steps leading into darkness, "you can visit where they conducted the examination that Hemingway mentions—but never describes—in *A Moveable Feast*."

The café did happen to be the original, but I could

have used another, and nobody would be the wiser. What mattered was the sense of reaching out and touching the past. After the first hour, the visitors moved more slowly, looked around more keenly, didn't simply peer into the street-level boutiques but raised their eyes to the windows of the first floor and wondered. . .

❊ · 25 · ❊

A Walk in the Earth

And the Lord said unto Satan, Whence comest thou?
Then Satan answered the Lord, and said,
From going to and fro in the earth, and
from walking up and down in it.

JOB 1:7

Hugo rang me one gray Sunday in the middle of my first spring in Paris.

Back in those days, before the arrival of Louise, Marie-Do and I lived in her tiny studio in Place Dauphine, on the Ile de la Cité. I spoke no French and knew nobody except for a few English-speakers rounded up by her compassionate family.

Of these relative strangers, the one I saw most was Hugo. A wolfish New Yorker in his late thirties, he appeared able to live in Paris without doing anything very much except for . . . well, some sort of writing. He was never very precise, and I didn't press, mostly in fear that he'd ask me to read something.

He'd been amiable enough when we met at the home of my sister-in-law, but his manner struck me as sinister. Probably his way of looking at one sideways, never directly, and communicating in a barely audible mumble. It fitted him perfectly to play Faulkner's "soiled man in a subway lavatory with a palm full of French post-cards."

Though Hugo set out to make me a friend, I never believed for a moment in his sincerity. At first I assumed he wanted an entrée to editors and agents for his mysterious literary efforts. As I got to know him better, other motives became more credible. He appeared to have cast me as a character in a psychodrama being played out in his mind. Expatriate fiction from Henry James to Patricia Highsmith seethes with such situations, but the closest parallel appeared to be that classic tale of expatriate betrayal, *The Third Man*. In this Parisian version, I was bumbling Holly Martins, writer of pulp westerns, adrift in postwar Vienna. Not speaking a word of the language, I was patronized and misled by smarter and more cunning locals, none more so than my supposed friend, suave, ruthless, philosophizing black marketer Harry Lime—embodied, naturally, in Hugo.

It was as Lime that Hugo rang me that afternoon. Marie-Do was at work and I'd been thinking about writing. Thinking was as far as it got. I felt numbed by the hollow booming of Notre Dame's bells, so unlike the clanging cheerfulness of English churches. The sense in Paris that one was wading through history, real and imagined, could depress you. Was there anything here that hadn't already been thought, written, done?

Hugo's call chimed exactly with my mood.

"What's happening?" he asked.

"Nothing. You?"

"Nothing. Wanna, uh, go someplace?"

"Like?"

"Oh . . . someplace. I gotta few ideas. See you at the Danton at two?"

At two, the overcast was, if anything, more oppressive. A wind drove the tourists in their beige Burberries through the square like dead leaves. I watched Hugo as he crossed boulevard Saint-Germain. His grubby sweater, baggy cords, and hand-knitted scarf fit right in. Ignoring the Paris tradition of scarfmanship, in which the way you wrapped, looped, hung, or draped the thing conveyed subtle hints about your character, profession, and sexual orientation, he wore both ends tucked down the front of the sweater, possibly the least attractive style short of a hangman's knot.

He didn't sit down.

"Let's go."

"Where?"

"You'll see."

His grin was malevolent. Had I been a woman, I'd have invented a headache. As it was, I walked to the corner with him and descended into the métro in the shadow of Danton's monument, erected, like most statues, long after it could have given the subject any satisfaction.

We emerged at Square Denfert-Rochereau, on the southern edge of old Paris, almost underneath another memorial, the bronze *Lion de Belfort*, a lion *couchant*, celebrating the inadequate defense of Paris against the Prussians in 1870. A few blocks farther down boulevard Saint-Michel, I'd often passed a modest stone plinth topped by the languid semireclining figure of a naked woman, holding her head, apparently in mild distress, as from a hangover. The wordy inscription explains that she commemorates the discovery of quinine as a defense against malaria. Obviously the size of statues in France is in inverse proportion to the achievement they celebrate.

OSSEMENTS DE L'ANCIEN
CIMETIÈRE DE LA MAGDELEINE
(RUE DE LA VILLE LÉVÊQUE N.ᵒˢ 1 et 2)
DÉPOSÉS EN 1844 DANS L'OSSUAIRE
DE L'OUEST ET TRANSFÉRÉS DANS LES
CATACOMBES EN SEPTEMBRE 1859.

The catacombs. "Here begins the empire of death."

In the shadow of the lion, two eighteenth-century customs houses marked where the city's inner walls once separated Paris proper from the countryside. Hugo led me across to one of them. We lined up at a tiny booth with shattered windows, paid ten francs, and were admitted through a door in a wooden wall painted deep, gloomy green. I puzzled out the water-stained sheet of official regulations framed behind dirty glass.

"The *Catacombs*?"

Hugo looked smug. He was enjoying this—so much, in fact, that he'd paid my admission himself—incredible munificence from someone who used a pocket calculator to split a café bill.

"What made you think I'd want to go down here?" The narrow concrete staircase spiraling into the earth hardly looked wide enough to admit our shoulders.

"It's interesting." Hugo grinned evily. "You'll love it."

"I don't think so." I read the wooden sign. "Sixty meters—that's almost two hundred feet."

"Writers should experience everything."

Hugo's sneer was infuriating. Grabbing a steel railing worn smooth by thousands of nervous hands, I joined the procession descending into the dark.

It took a long time. The grating of our soles on gritty concrete became increasingly loud. I was aware of my breath, and an oppressive heaviness and dampness.

At the bottom, we entered a long tunnel, so narrow that outstretched hands could touch both walls. Hugo had brought a flashlight. So had other visitors, obviously regulars like him. He turned it on the walls, where dressed stone slabs alternated with rock still bearing scars from the pick.

"It's quite safe," he said.

I told myself there was nothing sinister about this place. Strata of honey-colored sandstone underlay large areas of Paris, but in most places housing made open quarries impossible. Instead, since Roman times, the stonecutters had gone underground and tunneled, until northwestern Paris became honeycombed with their excavations.

The volume of rock weighed oppressively on my head. But I followed the jittering beam.

We walked for what felt like an hour down a passage that narrowed until two people couldn't have passed without turning sideways. The floor rose and fell. A thick black line ran along the roof just above our heads. It looked like the soot mark of a thousand torches, but I found later that it had been put there as a guide for nineteenth-century visitors. Periodically, I noticed passages, all closed off with locked metal gates. Hugo turned the flashlight into one of these caves. The light penetrated a few meters and was swallowed up.

As we penetrated farther, steel gates gave way to looping ironwork, painted in flaking white. Graffiti was cut into the walls, mostly names and years. The dates got older as we went farther in. 1876. 1814. 1787. Before the Germans. Before Napoleon. Before the Revolution.

The deeper we went, the less frequent became the electric lights, the more saturated the air. Droplets condensed on the ceiling and plashed to the floor. Finally, we reached a narrow door on the low lintel of which was carved "Ici Commence l'Empire de la Mort." Here begins the Empire of Death.

As an idea for relieving pressure on the city's overcrowded cemeteries, storing the bones in these caves dated back to the eighteenth century. But Haussmann's workmen were the first to do so systematically. Once they started excavating medieval Paris, they found cellars, graveyards, plague pits full of skeletons: a stratum of death. Instead of returning empty to the tunnels, the wagons carried the bones back to their quarries, where they reburied them, with due ceremony and not a little imagination.

The bones are there still, eleven kilometers of them, turned tobacco-colored by age and mold, and barely visible in the dark, packed head-high on both sides of the tunnel with bricklayer's care. A course of skulls, ten courses of femurs and tibias, then another course of skulls. When they got bored, or the quantity simply overwhelmed them, they heaped them wherever they could. Barred bays showed further corridors filled with skulls and pelvises, though in some places they'd spilled down as the ceiling gave way.

Stone slabs between the bays gave details of the churches from which the bones were brought, and meditations in French and Latin on the transitoriness of life. A few people even *chose* to be buried down here. They lay in white painted catafalques carved out of the rock.

We stood back to let another group pass. It's only since the 1960s that tourists have been admitted. Before then, nobody was allowed in, for fear of them wandering off into the dark. Today, thousands walk the tunnels every week—so many that, not long after our visit, they were closed for a major refurbishment, then shut again when vandals scattered bones and spray-painted graffiti.

Hugo leered at me from the dark. His torch lit his face eerily.

"So. Whaddya think?"

I told him what he wanted to hear. "Creepy."

"Yeah. Isn't it." Hugo beamed.

He was in his element down here. Visitors from the United States, lacking as long a history, were a pushover for stories of lost treasures, ancient mysteries, and haunted chateaux. *The Da Vinci Code* is just the latest in a succession of creepy Paris fantasies like

Notre-Dame de Paris, featuring the deaf hunchbacked bell ringer Quasimodo, the tales of black-masked villains like Fantomas and Judex, and the hugely popular *Phantom of the Opera*.

As late as the 1920s, the city didn't publicize the whereabouts of the catacombs. A 1927 book promising inside information about the *real* Paris treated the information almost as a state secret. "Few people you will meet in Paris can tell you where the Catacombs are located. Here is that coveted information. Taxi to corner of Place Denfert—and rue Rochereau." For those who hadn't read such books, guides offered what they claimed were clandestine visits. Clients were led through dark and smelly lanes to a gate beyond which narrow stone stairs and dripping tunnels brought them to a door with the painted sign CATACOMBS. PRIVATE PROPERTY. Under it, a faded coat of arms hinted at aristocracy. Inside, they found a cellar lined with skeletons, presided over by a distinguished bearded gentleman who graciously accepted a small fee (dollars preferred) to show them around. When a skeptic touched the suspiciously fresh-looking bones and found they were wax, the "Duc" explained the originals had long since crumbled into dust.

I'd lied when I told Hugo I found the experience macabre. The catacombs, like everything in France, were permeated with domesticity. Over the centuries, the quarrymen, typically French, made a little suburb of them. In the wall of a grotto, one had carved the façade of a model palace ten feet high. Dried green moss showed where a stream had once oozed out of the soft stone and washed down runnels into a now-dry pool. The national genius for evasion, accommodation, diplomacy, and disguise had been applied to death as well. Like oysters enrobing some irritating grit into a pearl, they lacquered a discomfiting object with layers of ritual and form. So respectfully arranged, the bones of the dead appeared no more gruesome than seashells edging a garden bed.

The path wound through and around the ancient workings. Sandstone isn't granite, and if you quarry too much in any one place it caves in, forming *cloches*—bells, conical domes fifty feet high. Sometimes the householders above only knew that mining was taking place below them when a pit opened and a house dropped out of sight. We passed through half a dozen of these natural domes and, protected from a nasty fall by a flimsy handrail, looked down on a hollow where a natural spring had been turned into a foot bath. Filtered through meters of rock, the water was colorless as air. Apparently some stonecutters, accustomed to murkier water, feared to wash in it. Anything so insubstantial was unnatural, likely cursed.

The public entrance was only one of hundreds. If you knew the right manholes, you could get in from anywhere under this part of Paris. Above the graffito "1786," a more recent visitor had added "1968" and the trefoil of the Campaign for Nuclear Disarmament. The catacombs attracted thrill seekers, devil worshippers, and plotters. It was here that the Marquis de Lafayette schemed to form a private army and sail to the aid of George Washington and the American rebels. The Resistance met here during World War II to plot sabotage of the occupying Nazis. Illegal parties were a tradition almost as old as the tunnels themselves. Modern geology students use them to celebrate their graduation. So did doctors; one manhole conveniently opened in a courtyard of a nearby hospital.

The official route led us back to another serpentine staircase and the welcome air and space of Denfert-Rochereau.

"We could go somewhere else next week." Hugo said with the eagerness of a kid on Halloween proposing some fresh infantile outrage. "I know lotsa good places."

"Like?"

"The sewers?"

❋ · 26 · ❋

Heaven and Hell

Who knows what evil lurks in the hearts of men?
The Shadow knows!
INTRODUCTION OF THE 1930S
RADIO SERIAL *The Shadow*

I never took up Hugo's invitation to tour *les égouts*. As I
found out later, one couldn't anyway, and hadn't been
able to since the 1970s. Up until then, husky employees of
the system would haul visitors in boats. After that, they
rode in carts attached to the wall, and then open carriages
drawn by a small locomotive, but even that's disappeared,
along with the pretext of a tour. Instead, an abandoned
part of the system under the Quai d'Orsay became the
Paris Sewer Museum. You can inspect sanitized and artfully lit tunnels and in one's imagination at least reenact
Jean Valjean's flight from Javert in *Les Misérables*.

Exhibits like this didn't lack visitors. The gothic novels of the eighteenth century gave rise to legends about devil worship in ancient crypts and nuns held prisoner by lubricious priests. The earliest tourists, particularly from the United States, arrived with the conviction that the Paris beneath their feet was inhabited by ghouls, grave robbers, and devil worshippers who roamed catacombs lined with bones, and that a hidden lake existed under the Paris Opera on which a malevolent musical genius poled himself, snatching the occasional straying soprano and carrying her to his lair.

Never slow to see a profit, cabarets in Montmartre and Montparnasse transformed themselves into nightclubs with fanciful names—The End of the World, The Dead Rat, The White Wolf, The Mad Cow. "Ghost show cabarets" flourished. A favorite was Le Cabaret du Néant, the Cabaret of Nothingness. As you entered, a voice boomed "Welcome, O weary wanderer, to the realm of death! Enter, choose your coffin, and be seated beside it." In the main bar, or *salle d'intoxication*, you sat at tables shaped like coffins, under chandeliers of human bones, while waiters dressed in the uniform of undertakers, with frock coats and top hats, brought you your drinks. Punters were then ushered into a narrow crypt,

Cabaret du Néant—the Cabaret of Nothingness

the "Room of Disintegration," and seated on narrow benches in the semidark. At the far end, an upright coffin contained the body of an apparently dead young woman, wrapped in a shroud. The lights dimmed...

Her face slowly became white and rigid; her eyes sank; her lips tightened across her teeth; her cheeks took on the hollowness of death—she was dead. But it did not end with that. From white the face slowly grew more livid ... then purplish-black.... The eyes visibly shrank into their greenish-yellow sockets.... Slowly the hair fell away.... The

nose melted away into a purple putrid spot. The
whole face became a semi-liquid mass of corruption.
Presently all this had disappeared, and a gleaming
skull showed where so recently had been the
handsome face of a woman.

Anyone who knew theater would have recognized Pepper's Ghost, which used carefully lighted and angled sheets of glass to create the illusion of a phantom. But most visitors were so impressed they contributed generously to the man who stood at the exit with an upturned skull, into which you were encouraged to drop a few coins of appreciation.

The prize for showmanship, however, went to twin establishments in Montmartre called Le Ciel (heaven) and L'Enfer (hell). Guides explained that the two enterprises, though sharing the same building, were run by different men—L'Enfer by a known criminal, and Le Ciel by a former crook who'd Seen the Light. Of course the same person owned both, the devils of one doubling as angels next door. Molded plasterwork decorated both frontages. For heaven, which promised "art and fun," a girl sat on a crescent moon being adored by a lover, while the door to hell took the form of a gaping mouth with goggling eyes and bared teeth.

Entrance to the Cabaret d'Enfer—the Cabaret of Hell

The doorman of hell was a devil with a pitchfork; for heaven, Saint Peter, a bearded giant holding a key as tall as himself.

Like all such shows, L'Enfer lectured new arrivals to put them in the correct state of mind. As they stepped inside the yawning mouth, the devil greeted them with "Enter, dear damned!" If there were women, it continued, "Come on, lovely impure ones. Take a seat, charming sinners. You will be roasted on both sides."

They sat at tables lit with red and green light, under statues showing souls writhing in hell, and gave their drinks orders to one of the imps who stood about with what looked like red-hot irons, with which they poked the clients. A black coffee with a cognac on the side became "A bumper of molten sins, with a dash of brimstone intensifier" and was served with a warning: "This will season your intestines, and render them invulnerable, for a time at least, to the tortures of the melted iron that will be soon poured down your throats." While waiting for damnation, they were entertained by, according to the program, "diabolical attractions, including the tortures of the damned, and the furnace." One of these was a pot in which two musicians, supposedly simmering for three thousand years, found the energy to play on a guitar and a mandolin.

Le Ciel, less seductive at first glance, placed you at a long table with men in ecclesiastical costume who offered "divine service, and sermon by the most humorous preacher in Paris." It became more interesting with "the monk's dream. Illustrated by *tableaux vivants* of the lusts of the flesh." After this, clients were invited to the first floor to enjoy "suave visions of celestial bliss, acrobatics by angels in the clouds. Metamorphosis of a lady spectator into an angel. (Safe return to former condition ensured.) Interesting experiments made with the assistance of gentlemen from the audience. Visions of Mahometan Paradise and oriental ecstasy."

Celestial bliss and oriental ecstasy—if only I could promise that to my walking clients. But it sounded like a tall order for just one person. As for spectators being made to disappear and reappear, for the moment, it'd be enough if my clients didn't follow those of Professor Andrew and simply melt away. I'd been lucky once. But a convenient opium pipe would not come along every day, and my stock of stories about Parisian vice and depravity would soon run dry. Some serious thought would be needed.

Blue Hour Blues

*I have drunk since I was fifteen and few things have
given me more pleasure. When you work hard all day
with your head and know you must work again the
next day, what else can change your ideas and make
them run on a different plane like whisky? When you
are cold and wet what else can warm you? Before an at-
tack who can say anything that gives you the momentary
well-being that rum does? The only time it isn't good
for you is when you write or when you fight. You have
to do that cold. But it always helps my shooting.
Modern life, too, is often a mechanical oppression
and liquor is the only mechanical relief.*

ERNEST HEMINGWAY

O**n the afternoon of my last walk for the seminar,
I found myself not far from where I'd abandoned
Hugo after our visit to the catacombs, at the intersec-

tion of boulevard du Montparnasse and the boulevard Saint-Michel. A current of nostalgia more powerful than the brisk rain-filled wind carried me across the street to shelter behind the hedges of the leafily secluded Closerie des Lilas.

The lunch crowd had gone home, and a few waiters were moving around the restaurant, setting tables for dinner. I turned left, past the grand piano where, in an hour, a pianist would be trifling with a repertoire of the Gershwins, Cole Porter, and Edith Piaf, and into the back bar.

A small brass plate inlaid in each table identifies a famous drinker who, in the golden days of the 1920s, could be found at this table or, occasionally, under it. Mine read MAN RAY—coincidentally the perfect choice, since Ray lived nearby, on rue du Val-de-Grâce, when he painted *A l'Heure de l'Observatoire, les Amoureux*, his image of a woman's red lips, big as an airship, floating over the dome of the observatory, just a block or two away.

I had the place almost to myself. Even the bar was untended. Two lovers cuddled in a corner, so entwined they appeared to have fused into a single entity. A lone drinker, slumped behind a cloudy yellow *pastis*, occupied the table I'd have preferred—the one with the brass plate reading ERNEST HEMINGWAY (better spelled than those for "Samuel Becket" and "Pierre Louis.")

Anglo-Saxon and Latin societies differ in their attitudes to the late afternoon. The English-speaking world assigns this time to the rush hour, drive time, or happy hour—a period to be blanked out, best forgotten, consigned to oblivion by boredom or booze, or the car radio tuned to the blur of back-to-back golden oldies. As Scott Fitzgerald said of Sunday in Hollywood, "not a day, but a gap between two other days."

In Italy, Spain, and France, a different reality obtains. In these countries, the evening hours between five and seven exist in a separate zone where time appears no longer to move, but hangs suspended, as the French say, *entre chien et loup*—between dog and wolf. Paris in particular welcomes the moment and wraps it in mythology and magic. For lovers, *le cinq à sept* is shorthand for that time they steal to be together—the hiatus between when one leaves work and the moment, two hours later, that one arrives home—if married, to eat with the family; if single, to feed the cat, mix a drink, take a bath, and remember.

Photographers and cinematographers call this time, particularly in late summer, "the magic hour." Sunlight, striking obliquely, and softened by longer progress through the air, is at its most flattering. Actresses have been known to throw after-lunch tantrums, develop headaches, or lock themselves in their caravans, only to recover and emerge, ready for their close-up, as the clock strikes five. Painters and poets prefer it in autumn, when the sky over Paris becomes a study in gray and rose, an invitation to melancholy. It inspired one of Verlaine's most famous poems, "Chanson d'Automne":

> *The long sighs*
> *Of the violins*
> *Of autumn*
> *Wound my heart*
> *With monotonous languor.*

It is also the time when perfumiers gather flowers, knowing their scent will be at its most powerful. Guerlain, having created a heady mixture of rose, iris, jasmine, vanilla, and musk, gave it the name by which this time is traditionally known, L'Heure Bleue—the blue hour.

Paris has inspired the world's saddest stories, and *l'heure bleue* more than its share, including *Babylon Revisited*, Fitzgerald's pastel sketch of the autumnal

city as seen through the eyes of an expatriate who returns after having drunk away his money, his family,
and his work.

> *Outside, the fire-red, gas-blue, ghost-green signs*
> *shone smokily through the tranquil rain. It was late*
> *afternoon and the streets were in movement; the*
> *bistros gleamed. At the corner of the boulevard des*
> *Capucines he took a taxi. The Place de la Concorde*
> *moved by in pink majesty; they crossed the logical*
> *Seine, and Charlie felt the sudden provincial*
> *quality of the Left Bank. Charlie directed his taxi*
> *to the Avenue de l'Opéra, which was out of his way.*
> *But he wanted to see the blue hour spread over the*
> *magnificent façade.*

Charlie returns in the hope of retrieving his child.
It's certain he'll fail, since failure is the only thing for
which he's shown an aptitude. We also know he will go
back to the bottle, as did Fitzgerald himself. For some
writers, drink is not an escape but a career.

It's said that anything true written about Hollywood
in the 1970s must acknowledge the importance of

cocaine. Expatriate Paris in the 1920s only makes sense if we recognize the centrality of booze.

The Volstead Act of 1920 made it illegal to sell alcohol in the United States. Not in Europe, of course. "To a certain class of American," wrote Jimmie Charters, barman at the Dingo and the Jockey in Montparnasse, and later at Harry's Bar across the river, next to the Opéra, "drinking in excess became an obligation. No party was a success without complete intoxication of the guests."

For Paris's restaurateurs and barmen, booze was a bonanza. Before 1920, the French had barely heard of cocktails. They drank wine or beer, aperitifs before dinner, and digestifs afterward. Prohibition changed that. Cafés reopened as *bars américains*, with barmen, usually African Americans who had stayed on after the war, serving martinis, old-fashioneds, and whiskey sours. "Cocktails! That is the real discovery of our age," wrote Sisley Huddlestone, correspondent of the London *Times*, in 1928, when he interviewed one of the most popular painters in Montparnasse.

> *[Kees] van Dongen, the most Parisian of Dutch painters, whom I remember as a struggling, not to say starving artist in Montparnasse, but who*

*has now become a rich portraitist holding eccentric
but fashionable midnight parties, stroked his big
blond beard, reflected a moment and then with
a twinkle in his eye delivered his epigram. "Our
epoch," he said, "is the cocktail epoch. Cocktails!
They are of all colours. They contain something
of everything. No, I do not mean merely the
cocktails one drinks. They are symbolic of the rest.
The modern society woman is a cocktail. She is a
bright mixture. Society itself is a bright mixture.
You can blend people of all tastes and classes. The
cocktail epoch!"*

Paris was one big and boozy party. Paul Morand in
1930 noticed the popularity of the Saltrates Rodell, a
patented foot bath, perfect for soaking your aching soles
after a night of dancing the Charleston.

For café owners, the investment more than paid off.
Foreigners liked to drink early, in the late afternoon,
when French customers were still at work and the cafés
would normally be empty. They also ate early, unlike
the French, who seldom sat down before nine. Above
all, they possessed unquenchable thirsts. The French
drank for pleasure and relaxation; the Americans, the
Spaniards, and the Germans did so to get drunk. Order-

ing expensive mixed drinks or champagne, they sluiced them down, and demanded more, paying so readily they seldom noticed how flagrantly they were overcharged or shortchanged.

Even the most staid American visitor thought it a duty, on arriving in Paris, to get good and plastered (or squiffy, ginned, edged, jingled, potted, hooted, tanked, crocked, embalmed, lit like Macy's window, fried to the hat, or any one of sixty other synonyms helpfully listed by a 1927 guidebook). Young journalist Waverley Root, arriving to take a job on the *Herald Tribune*'s Paris edition, ordered a bottle of Bordeaux with his first meal on French soil. The waiter didn't explain that even the French don't drink with breakfast. Why would he? Business was business.

The likelihood that everyone was permanently drunk accounts for the joyous Paris of the 1920s as described in postwar memoirs like Morley Callaghan's *That Summer in Paris*, Sylvia Beach's *Shakespeare and Company*, and above all Hemingway's *A Moveable Feast*. Contemporary descriptions are nowhere near as enthusiastic. They make those famous bars sound squalid. The Dingo, where Hemingway and Fitzgerald first met, was small, noisy, and noted for the eccentricity of its clients: "dingo" was a corruption of *dingue*—crazy. Explaining why he called his memoirs *This Must Be the Place*, its barman, Jimmie Charters, recalled:

> *I remember one time walking from the Dôme to the Dingo. Ten feet or so ahead of me was Flossie Martin. As she came abreast of the bar entrance, a handsome Rolls Royce drove up to the curb and from it stepped two lavishly dressed ladies. For a moment they hesitated. They looked at the Dingo questioningly. They peered in the windows between the curtains.*
>
> *Flossie, seeing them, looked her contempt. As she passed into the bar she tossed a single phrase over her shoulder.*
>
> *"You bitch!"*
>
> *Whereupon the lady so addressed nudged her companion anxiously.*
>
> *"Come on, Helen," she said. "This must be the place!"*

One guidebook called the Jockey "indescribable." It had "low, cracked ceilings and the tattered walls covered with posters. Cartoons painted with shoe polish." Harry's was a dingy tourist trap where they watered the liquor and stole your change. As if it wasn't already suf-ficiently *déclassé*, in 1924 it launched the International Bar Flies association. For $1, members got a badge—two flies in top hats, buzzing at one another—and were taught the code of recognition. "Flick a member on the left shoulder as if a fly were there, give him the grip which is natural to all I.B.Fs— the right hand extended as if holding a glass of whiskey, the right foot raised the height of a bar rail—and *buzz*."

All the same, drunks like Scott Fitzgerald became maudlin when they recalled barmen who, with the sun barely above the horizon, would prepare an eye-opener to numb the effects of a hangover. Compli-ments might have been fewer had the drinkers known how they were being exploited. Jimmie Charters con-fessed in his memoirs (for which Hemingway wrote an introduction) that his salary was the smallest part of his income.

*A barman makes his real profit from the tips. . . .
[Also] professional services [are] offered free by
doctors, lawyers, and others among his clients.
Then, too, in France he obtains reduced rates at the
theater and cinemas, and some less-distinguished
night-life resorts. When we steered clients to such*

HARRY'S NEW YORK BAR

5, Rue Daunou - PARIS

(Opera district)   Tél: OPE. 73-00

Same location 52 Years
Just tell the taxi-driver

« SANK ROO DOE NOO »

Card for Harry's Bar, watering hole of international barflies

*places, we received up to 60 per-cent commission,
and there was always 25 per-cent commission from
gambling houses, as well as free meals and drinks
when we called. The barman also gets a small
commission from the French liquor people: a franc a
bottle for gin, brandy, and whisky, fifty centimes to
a franc for bar champagne, up to five francs for the
expensive champagne in the cabarets, and twenty-
five centimes on everything else.*

French bars found even more cunning methods
of swindling customers. Expatriate publisher Nancy
Cunard and two friends ordered gin fizzes at a café on
boulevard Saint-Michel but found them undrinkable.
Once the owner produced the gin bottle, they understood. The label said AMERICAN GIN. Not content with
distributing their bathtub mixtures in the domestic
market, the bootleggers had got into export.

I know you," said an American voice, interrupting
my musing.

It was the man who'd been drinking *pastis*. Belat-
edly I recognized Andrew, the academic I'd replaced as
guide.

"I went on one of your walks," I reminded him.

"Yes, of course . . ." He made the connection. "Oh, and you took over from me."

"Well, Dorothy said . . . some health problem . . . ? "

"Oh, I don't mind. I was grateful, to tell the truth. Mind if I sit down?"

He subsided into the seat opposite. Out of the sun, he looked less young. Nor, I intuited, was that *pastis* his first of the day.

"I *knew* I was being boring," he said, with the frankness most drinkers believe is disarming but is mostly just embarrassing. "But teaching college gets you into bad habits. *You* know what it's like. Students who haven't read anything older than the last vampire novel. . . . You get used to explaining *everything*."

In her novel *Foreign Relations*, Alison Lurie's American academic in London visualizes self-pity as a sad dog that follows her about. As Andrew talked, I felt the snuffling of his particular pooch and patted it under the table. How exactly he fitted the pattern of those intellectuals who came to Paris, intent on making their name and, disillusioned, settled instead into monosyllabic misery, fed by booze. James Wood, writing about Richard Yates, creator of the bleak *Revolutionary Road*, and a member of the Montparnasse Class of '51, evoked a series of "homes identical in their shabby discipline of neglect. In each there was a table for writing, a circle of crushed cockroaches around the desk chair, curtains made colorless by cigarette smoke, a few books, and nothing much in the kitchen but coffee, bourbon, and beer."

Changing the subject, I said, "No coincidence we should run into one another here." Looking round, I went on, "This must be the place."

It was the wrong thing to say. Data bubbled out unstoppably.

"Ah, you're thinking of Harry's Bar. Jimmie Charters was at the Dingo, not here. And after that at the Jockey, then Harry's, 5 rue Danou. . . ." He gave a patronizing little laugh. "Or, as they used to spell it out, phonetically, for those who didn't speak French, 'Sank Roo Doe Noo.' Hemingway drank here at the Closerie, of course. And wrote too—*Big Two Hearted River*, for instance. But Charters . . ."

"Let me get you another." I said hurriedly. "*Pastis*, is it?"

"Oh, yes. Thanks." Then he was off again. "Though I suppose it should be a Montgomery . . ."

The Montgomery martini was a Hemingway invention: fifteen parts of gin to one of vermouth—the supe-

riority of troops under his command that Field Marshal
Bernard Montgomery required before he would fight.

"Maybe later," I said, imagining the effect. "For the
moment, I'll stick to Campari and orange."

The barman took our order. In the days of Hemingway and Fitzgerald, he'd have been confidant, confes-
sor, co-conspirator, pimp. Today, he also served as
historical source. In documentaries about Hemingway,
waiters and hoteliers chat as if he'd been an old friend.
"Sure. Papa came in here all the time . . ." When he died,
French TV rounded up three authorities to summarize
his life: a bullfighter, Sylvia Beach—and the barman at
the Ritz.

Nobody mentioned the inconvenient fact that, before
World War II, Hemingway almost never visited the
Ritz. For a start, it was on the Right Bank, far from "the
Quarter." As a struggling writer in the 1920s, he might
have come if invited and someone else was picking up
the tab, but normally he couldn't afford its prices, which
were—and remain—astronomical. When he did have
money, he preferred the Crillon, looking out on Place
de la Concorde.

Nevertheless, after his death the Ritz canonized him
as its patron saint, even to creating a Hemingway Bar.
It's artfully done: a bronze portrait head, photographs

from *les années folles*, a few books for added color. Supposedly writers can even have their mail sent there, as used to be the case at the Dôme and the Rotonde, which kept racks by the door for that purpose. But Hemingway never drank in the bar that bears his name. In his time, it was the Ladies Bar, a ghetto for the women who, in those days, were excluded from the big bar. "A tiny box-like room," jeered one 1927 guidebook, "scarcely more than fifteen feet square . . . densely packed [with] American flappers, cinema queens, stage belles and alimony spenders." Another christened it "the Black Hole of Calcutta . . . the steam room" and noted that "about six o'clock at night, the place is filled to suffocation and has a delicate perfume faintly reminiscent of attar of roses in a bottle of old Bourbon." If you like ironies, in 1997, Princess Diana, fleeing the paparazzi by using the side entrance, hurried past this former shrine of misogyny en route to her death.

The Ritz and Hemingway only embraced one another after 1944. After "liberating" the Odéon, he led his group across the Seine, gathering members as he went, until more than seventy invaded the Ritz bar. According to tradition, Hemingway ordered Montgomeries all round. A grateful management installed him in one of its best suites, on the inner side overlooking the courtyard, and catered to his every whim. His mistress and later wife, Mary Welsh, moved in next door, and it was supposedly in the basement of the hotel that, decades later, she found the suitcases containing the "forgotten" manuscripts that became, among other books, *A Moveable Feast*.

It was Scott Fitzgerald, not Hemingway, who made the Ritz and its bar legendary. He used it for scenes in *Tender Is the Night* and a number of short stories, in particular the elegaic *Babylon Revisited*, and routinely drank himself insensible there—no struggle, since he would, as one friend wrote, dissolve in alcohol like a paper flower after only two or three drinks. When *Gatsby* was back in print and his star was on the rise, visitors to the Ritz asked about Fitzgerald, but nobody remembered just another drunk. In *A Moveable Feast*, the barman even asks Hemingway "Papa, who is this Mr. Fitzgerald who everyone asks me about? It is strange that I have no memory of him." But, acknowledging that a barman is just as ready to whip up an anecdote as a cocktail, he confesses that he tells them "anything interesting they will wish to hear; what will please them."

Hem and his cronies would have sneered at my caution about spending the rest of the evening getting drunk. And I agree it was tempting, in the cozy companionship of the Closerie des Lilas, to order a round of Montgomeries, then another and another. The barman, loyal to his craft, would keep them coming, along with salty nuts and crisps to maintain our thirst. Once the pianist arrived, we'd soon be cocking our heads and nodding in recognition of *The Last Time I Saw Paris* or *Mad About the Boy*. Predinner couples would fill the remaining tables—including perhaps some people we knew, who'd join us, and we'd call to the barman, *"M'sieur, s'il vous plaît, encore la même chose . . ."* And then, in the long inglorious tradition of *l'heure bleue*, the night would be drowned and lost.

· 28 ·

The Last of Montparnasse

We slid down the hill to 1939 the way the period
of the nineties slid down to 1914. We sank into
the abyss as into some kind of pleasure.

PAUL MORAND

*I*n summer, the cafés of Paris fold back their glass walls so that one sits on the sidewalk, with pedestrians brushing your tiny table, sometimes rattling your *eau à la menthe* or jangling the coffee cups. Apologies can end in an invitation to sit down and share a drink, and occasionally even more.

Not surprisingly, Gelenter was to be found every summer morning at Deux Magots, eyes darting among the passing women, body poised and ready, given the slightest encouragement, to bolt after one of them.

"You look just like our cat," I said. "He quivers that way when he's stalking a bird."

"Mmm?"

"Nothing. You said you had an idea?"

He dragged his mind back from the turn of an ankle, the play of muscle under a tight skirt, the tremble of a breast.

"Oh, yeah. Some people who've taken the Odéon walk want to know if you do any others. Around Montparnasse, maybe, so I was thinking . . . art?"

I could see why art looked like a logical choice for a walk.

At the turn of the twentieth century, every artist wanted to study in Paris. They flocked here. The Académie des Beaux Arts and private schools like the Académie Julienne and the Académie de la Grande Chaumière could barely keep up. So many students crammed into the life class at Julienne, all puffing self-importantly on pipes, that those at the back complained they couldn't see the model for smoke. Artists colonized Montparnasse and Montmartre. The cafés overflowed with painters and models. Their annual Bal des Quat'z Arts—the Ball of the Four Arts—was legendary for the costumes of the men and the nudity of the models, among whom anything more than a coat of body paint was looked on as overdressing. "The students are the pets of Paris," said one indulgent writer in 1899. He even justified the Bal des Quat'z Arts as educational: "Its marvellous brilliancy, its splendid artistic effects, and its freedom and abandon, has a stimulating and broadening effect of the greatest value to art. The artists and students see in these annual spectacles only grace, beauty, and majesty; their training in the studios, where they learn to regard models merely as tools of their craft, fits them, and them alone, for the wholesome enjoyment of the great ball."

Painting became a spectator sport. The competitive shows, called *salons*, were as much social occasions as the races at Longchamps. It was particularly *à la mode* to attend the preview, known as a *vernissage*, or "varnishing," after the custom of allowing an artist a last chance to retouch his work. For the *vernissage* of the biggest event, the Salon des Artistes Français, fashionable Paris turned out en masse. A painting of 1911 shows the glass-roofed Grand Palais at the foot of the Champs-Elysées, cavernous as a railroad terminal, crammed with gorgeously gowned women and men sweating in formal dress. Here and there, a life-size statue lifts its head above the swirling, chattering mass, unacknowledged and ignored. Whatever these people were there for, it wasn't to admire the art.

Except for fashionable portraitists, few artists were rich. For the truly creative, the pleasure was in doing it; money was a by-product. Before starting work each morning, Renoir or Cézanne would dash off a few little watercolors "to get their hand going" and use them later to light the fire. Renoir, painting in the countryside with Cézanne, asked if he had something to use as toilet paper. Cézanne handed him a watercolor, which Renoir had already crumpled to wipe himself before he thought

A vernissage, *or private view, in the Grand Palais, 1890s*

to take a look. Once he did, he decided it was too good to waste. Ironed out, it hung in the Hollywood home of his filmmaker son Jean, a reminder that works of art hadn't always carried a price tag.

But run-of-the-mill painters extracted every franc from their work. They'd produce as many copies of a canvas as people would pay for, at different sizes to order. Gertrude Stein, looking at some paintings, remarked that the legs in one canvas didn't please her. "Cut them off if you like," urged the dealer. "The artist won't mind. He just wants the money." For these artists, the 1920s were a bonanza. Tourism flourished, and tourists wanted souvenirs. In 1928, Sisley Huddlestone complained about Montparnasse tours that offered a visit to "a real artist's studio."

At the top of some ricketty stairs, the guide pushed open an attic door to surprise a model posing naked while the artist daubed at a smeary canvas. While the painter protested and the model fled, the punter offered profuse apologies and, to cover his embarrassment, showed an exaggerated interest in the artist's work. Before long, the guide hinted that the painter might part with his masterpiece at wholesale rates. Half an hour later, the visitor left with the canvas under his arm, sure he had a bargain. The guide hung back to collect his cut, after which the model made coffee while her lover propped another old canvas on the easel, daubed some fresh paint on it, and awaited the next tour.

Worse, in Huddlestone's eyes, was the fact that serious artists were involved. Tsuguhara Foujita, Moïse Kisling, and Jules Pascin were inspired self-publicists. Foujita arrived at a Montparnasse ball mostly naked, to show off his tattoos, and trailing a wicker cage containing his wife, Fernande, likewise lightly clothed in not much more than a hair ribbon. The sign on the cage read WOMAN FOR SALE. Such a lifestyle left the Montparnos chronically short of funds, which they remedied by hectic salesmanship. Salvador Dalí was shameless. He'd arrive at the crowded La Coupole with a canvas under his arm and prowl the tables for a buyer.

André Breton had launched surrealism as a literary movement, but it soon belonged to the artists like Man Ray, de Chirico, Magritte, and in particular Dalí. As the young Spaniard hijacked his ideas and announced himself as surrealism's creator, Breton despairingly assigned the avaricious upstart the anagramatic nickname "Avida Dollars." Dalí left for the United States, and the art market followed.

It's hard to feel censorious about the painters of

The painter Foujita, a classic Montparno

Montparnasse in the 1920s. What Roger Shattuck wrote of the period before 1914 is just as true of the decade after 1918: "The cultural capital of the world, which set fashion in dress, the arts, and the pleasures of life, celebrated its vitality over a long table laden with food and wine." Theirs was the art of the brothels, cafés and streets; art that didn't take itself too seriously, and, above all, reflected appetite, not intellect. They became known as the School of Paris because the city and its citizens were their preferred subject. Earlier painters had gone to the country, believing truth lay in nature, but the Montparnos, as they were now being called, had no time for landscapes. They preferred people—either flamboyantly costumed or nude, and invariably behaving badly. Foujita threw scandalous costume parties. Francis Picabia loved fast cars. Many smoked opium or drank absinthe. Fifty years later, the same self-destructive spirit flourished in New York with the Beats, Andy Warhol's Factory, Punk.

Occasionally, I caught a whiff of those days. While researching a biography of Federico Fellini, I tracked one of his actresses, Marika Rivera, to her disordered studio in suburban London. Proudly, she reminded me her father was the Mexican painter Diego Rivera, and her mother the Russian artist Marevna, one of the mistresses-cum-models who became poster girls of *les années folles*. Marevna painted a group portrait of their circle—Rivera, Soutine, Kisling, Modigliani. It includes the young Marika. I tried to reconcile that solemn little girl with Astrodi, the heavy-bosomed middle-aged whore she plays in *Casanova*. During the production in Rome, Fellini, entertaining a group of money men at Cinecittà, invited Marika and some other actors to join them at lunch. As the food was served, he unexpectedly asked her to "bless the meal." After a few hints, she realized he wanted her to open her bodice and let her enormous breasts dangle over the table.

"Is there such a custom in Italy?" I asked.

"Not that I ever heard of."

"What did you do?"

She gave me the only answer one would expect from a Montparno. "Oh, just as he asked, of course." Placing her fingers between her breasts, she mimed ripping apart her blouse. "He was the *maestro*, after all."

I almost heard the collective gasp as the cornucopia of her bosom spilled out, putting into the shade the *fettucini al forno* and *vitello con funghi*. Fellini knew his audience. After a show like that, they wouldn't dare refuse him anything.

29

The Fuzz on the Peach

*A normal man, given a group photograph of school
girls and asked to point out the loveliest one, will not
necessarily choose the nymphet among them.*

VLADIMIR NABOKOV, *Lolita*

Although Gelenter's idea for a guided tour about
art seemed simple enough, I found it hard to
come up with a structure.

"It depends what sort of art you were thinking of."

"Oh, you know. Kiki of Montparnasse, surrealism,
Picasso. Modigliani . . . all that stuff."

"Great idea—except that the surrealists met in
Montmartre. They almost never came to Montparnasse.
And Picasso lived in the Marais . . ."

He dismissed my objections with a you're-not-
getting-it look.

"Suggest something else then."

"Forget the whole thing?"

"Nah." This was too good a plan to abandon just because it wasn't true. "There must be somewhere that artists still hang out."

I could think of only one place in Paris where greed, lust, and art cohabited in the great tradition of the 1900s, and while it was only a pale shadow of the old days, it did preserve a scrap of that naked venality.

"I *could* take them down rue Mazarine."

Jules Mazarin was a seventeenth-century cardinal, a protégé of Cardinal Richelieu. He inherited his role as first minister of France, but also his hunger for beautiful objects. An obsessive collector, with a particular penchant for diamonds, he kept his collections in his palace, the gilded dome of which, now the Institut de France, sits at the foot of the street named for him, proof that, though you can't take it with you, it's possible to leave an elegant souvenir.

A walk down rue Mazarine gives a good sense of what's going on in Paris's art world. If you try it on any Thursday evening, you'll find, particularly in summer, that a few galleries are hosting *vernissages*. Generally they don't mind if you wander in, accept a glass of wine, and eavesdrop on the conversation. If they do look askance, simply ask to see the price list. Even the hint of a sale makes the thorniest gallerist more amiable.

Though a few run to a second floor, most galleries are shoeboxes. You enter sideways and peer at the paintings with your nose almost touching the canvas. And the art? Expect to be bewildered, by variety if not talent. Abstracts by an unknown Rumanian follow canvases by a Spaniard who paints only rearing horses straddled by nude males. Tucked into a cobbled courtyard, a gallery shows some Jean Cocteau drawings a little too Cocteau-esque to be believable. Opposite is a shop filled with African masks and idols that haven't traveled farther than a garage in Belleville.

Erotica once was the Montparnos' hottest seller. In the 1920s, Pascin, Foujita, Kisling, and their colleagues pumped it out: on canvas for the carriage trade, but also as etchings and lithographs or expensively printed illustrated books with texts never meant to be read. Couturier Paul Poiret dressed the emancipated woman of the time in beautiful clothes so that Moïse Kisling could undress her to be painted.

To be painted nude was a badge of emancipation. The film star Arletty posed nude for Kisling. Man Ray, being American, and a natural entrepreneur, did a thriving under-the-counter trade in salacious photographs, often shot to order. For models, he used his own mistresses, like Kiki and Lee Miller, or the wives of friends, sometimes even an artist in her own right, such as Meret Oppenheim. Occasionally, Ray participated in person. Some things haven't changed. Mazarine galleries often show flagrantly sexual images by photographers Nobuyoshi Araki or Kohei Yoshiyuki, or the collages of fetish artist Pierre Molinier, who enjoyed being photographed in black lingerie and high heels, with a long-stemmed rose up his rectum.

Sex played its part in one of my most vivid memories of art and rue Mazarine. Passing one summer morning, I found a gallery open, and a new show of photographs being hung. The photographer—call him Julian Templeton—was English. I knew his work, but it took a few moments to realize the gray-haired man in crumpled white linen was the artist himself.

Templeton's trademark is soft-focus color photographs of teenage girls. Long-limbed, languid, and nude, bathed in golden light, they recline in haylofts or Provençal bedrooms furnished with Victorian china and bunches of violets. If lesbian activity had not recently taken place, it is about to. Licensing his images for use in everything from soap ads to jigsaw puzzles had made Templeton rich. But respectability is more elusive, so periodically he staged shows in Tokyo or Paris, where, unlike London, he didn't risk being picketed by anti-pedophile protestors or shut down by the police.

For this exhibition, in a further appeal for acceptance, he'd included lithographs by other, earlier artists who'd also used young girls as models. I knew one of these images, of two girls coiled on a sofa in a clinging *soixante-neuf*, and was peering at it, trying to figure out if it was an original, when he joined me.

"Gerda Wegener," I said. The Danish illustrator

One of Gerda Wegener's erotic lithographs

had been a sensation in 1920s Montparnasse, not least because of her unconventional lifestyle. Her husband Einar, who modeled for both her male and female figures, became one of the first men to undergo a successful surgical sex change.

"Yes! You're an artist?"

"Writer."

"A *writer*. How interesting. What might I have read of yours?"

Half an hour later, we were sitting on the terrace of a café on the Carrefour de Buci.

"I've been doing a little writing myself," he said. "Nothing too ambitious. Just a few experiments. Would you mind casting a professional eye over them?"

"Well, of course. Just send them . . ."

"Oh, I have them here." He produced a folder with some typed sheets.

I skimmed them. There was a lot about the dew on the mossy lip of the stream, a pearl nestling in its nacreous cup, the fawn bending shyly to sip. . .

"Erm . . ." Bypassing literary criticism, I went straight to the problems of publication. "Not easy to find a home for this kind of material. The market is nervous about anything so . . ." I scrambled for the suitable word. " . . . specialized."

"So I've found!" said Templeton. "No London publisher would even consider it. The British simply don't understand such things. Do you know, there isn't even a word in English for the kind of women I like?"

We ambled back to the gallery, where Templeton generously presented me with a copy of his memoirs, illustrated with more images of drowsing adolescents. He inscribed it, "To John Baxter, a member of the club."

That night, Neil Pearson, actor and biliophile, came to dinner. He leafed through the book and raised his eyebrows at the dedication. I mentioned Templeton's complaint about there being no word in English for girls of the kind who modeled for him.

"How about 'children'?" Neil said.

30

To Market

marché d'aligre
informations—fleurs
poissonniers—fruits
charcutiers—chalands*
fromager—fripes
caves—legumes
bouchers—balayage

aligre market
information—flowers
fishmongers—fruit
delicatessen—barges*
cheesemonger—old clothes
winery—vegetables
butchers—hair-coloring

SIGN AT ENTRANCE OF MARCHÉ D'ALIGRE

(*Chalands—"barges"—is slang for customers.)

*F*ew pleasures are more satisfying than strolling through a French market on a sunny day, pausing to chat with the vendors, enjoying a sample of some particularly tempting fruit or vegetable, and lingering over your choice of the most succulent items on sale.

Just don't expect this at Aligre.

One guidebook observes nervously of the market: "The diverse nature of this neighbourhood makes itself evident here." I would put it more strongly. Aligre is a zoo, a battlefield, a shouting match, a souk. A clash of cultures. If the old market of Les Halles was "the guts of Paris," this is the mouth, permanently agape, to taste and to bawl.

The heart of Aligre is an ancient roofed, stone-floored market with permanent shops selling cheese, meat, and fish at supermarket prices. Go there if you want, but to do so is to miss the real action on the square outside, where merchants sell cheap-but-cheery clothing, sunglasses, electrical goods, stockings. There's a *brocante* too, a flea market offering the usual miscellany of discarded utensils, ancient magazines, collections of anonymous snapshots, prints, and posters, among which may be found a rarity, even a treasure.

But above all this is a market for food. Many of the clients are Muslims, since it's the best inner-city source of halal meat, particularly lamb, but also chicken, preferred for slow cooking in tajines, and the thin merguez sausages of North Africa, deep red with paprika and chili. Restaurateurs shop here because a quarter sheep or a whole beef rump costs what a chichi butcher in the *seizième* would demand for a *gigot* or a kilo of *entrecote*.

Aligre's butchers are masters of skills that big-city butchers no longer practice. They sell lamb's kidneys, still embedded in the thick white suet that makes delicious pastry, and whole beef kidneys, for braising with mustard or madeira. They expertly and uncomplainingly bone your shoulder of lamb to be stuffed and rolled; trim your *entrecote*, leaving just the right amount of fat to lubricate it on the grill; slice a veal shin in perfect rounds for *osso bucco,* or without meat for use as *os à moelle*—marrow bones. Baked dry until the marrow starts to deliquesce into fat, they're served as an appetizer with coarse salt and thin dry toast.

Aligre is your one-stop market for anything to do with Mediterranean and Middle Eastern cooking: aubergines, courgettes, onions, carrots, garlic, tomatoes, coriander, basil, mint. The rule is, "Pile it high and sell it cheap." Forget about buying just one aubergine or a couple of tomatoes; all prices are for a kilo or, more often, two, and as noon approaches, when the market closes, selling becomes frantic. "Three kilos for one!" they yell, hoping to clear their stock. "A dozen for a euro!" Bags are shoveled to overflowing with strawberries or chilis or baby potatoes. Unloading your purchases in the kitchen later, you gape at the quantities. How am I going to use up twenty baby aubergines or two pounds of ripe cherries—and why did I buy all that coriander? But it was just so *cheap*. . .

For a while, the Australian chef Jean-Claude Bruneteau ran his little restaurant the Bennelong just around the corner. I visited Aligre with him and watched as he stroked an aubergine like a woman's cheek, weighed a fresh peach like a breast, ran his fingers through bunches of fresh parsley, marjoram, and tarragon as through a mane of hair. "I've never had such sweet strawberries," he said, his voice vivid with delight. "Juicy pineapples, ripe bananas, ripe tomatoes. No hydroponic lettuce. Six kinds of butter to choose from. No margarine in sight. It's food heaven here, really. Gorgeous, gorgeous, *gorgeous* food."

31

The Boulevard
of Crime

*A long boulevard, lined all the way with high, blank,
very grim walls, darkened by the chestnut trees then
newly planted, with very dim gas-lamps far distant one
from the other. . . . Fifty yards behind my back, running
footsteps sounded. . . . When they were very close, I ran
like hell. But they gained and gained on me. And they
gained. I stood at bay under a gas-lamp, beneath the
black walls of the prison.*

They emerged from the gloom—two men.

They ran on.

*They were apaches all right; there were the casquettes
with the visors right down over the eyes; the red
woollen mufflers floated out, the jackets were skintight,
the trousers ballooned out round the hips, and
one of them had an open jack knife.*

FORD MADOX FORD, *A Mirror to France*, 1926

While Hemingway enjoyed his cognac in La Coupole and the Fitzgeralds caroused at the Ritz, the boulevards seethed with larceny. It was only to the pampered *intellos* that Paris in the 1920s was indolent and tranquil. Just a few blocks from the lights of boulevard du Montparnasse, a different Paris began, which most tourists only glimpsed from the safety of a tour bus or read about in pulp novels featuring avengers like Fantomas and Judex who stalked the roofs of Paris in opera capes, top hats, and black domino masks.

Americans shrugged off the seedy side of Paris. It didn't interest them that *poules* cruised Montparnasse outside the big cafés, that their *mecs* openly sold heroin and cocaine, known locally as *chnouf*, or that knifings and shootings took place every night. Thanks to Prohibition, the United States had more crime than it could handle. They preferred things that were rarer back home—sex, alcohol, and art.

To tourists from more disciplined nations, however, in particular Germany and Russia, crime was pornography, and they couldn't get enough. In particular they admired the street gangsters known as *apaches*—to rhyme with "crash." Why they adopted this name is obscure. They may have admired the stone-faced braves brought to Paris by Wild West shows like that of Buffalo Bill

Cody. Another explanation traces the name to a news-paper report of a Montmartre brawl, where the journal-ist wrote, "The fury of a riotous incident between two men and a woman rose to the ferocity of savage Apache Indians in battle."

Like all street gangs, *les apaches* took fancy names, conducted elaborate initiations, and affected a uniform. You knew an *apache* from his striped jersey, tight jacket, and flat peaked cap, tilted low over his eyes. A red wool sash served as a scarf in cold weather and doubled as a mask. In the 1932 film *Love Me Tonight*, Maurice Che-valier, a tailor passing himself off as a baron, puts on a similar outfit to sing the Rodgers and Hart song "Poor Apache." His aristo hosts shiver in delight as he prances around the great hall, his shadow enormous on the wall, boasting, "The thing that makes me happy / Is to make a woman cry . . . When I take her wrist and twist it / No woman can resist it." He calls his sweetheart "a shop girl" and "a treasure," but in explaining that she makes him "a gentleman of leisure," we're meant to know she's a whore and he is her pimp.

In 1901, two *apache* gang leaders, Leca and Manda, fought over such a girl, a teenage prostitute, Amélie Hélie, whose blond hair earned her the name Casque d'Or—"Golden Helmet." Leca died, and Manda was

An apache, *the Paris gangster of the 1900s*

guillotined in the yard of the Santé Prison. According to legend, Amélie watched her lover's execution from one of the windows overlooking the prison that locals rented to ghoulish thrill-seekers. "Poor Apache" evokes their story. Chevalier assumes he will end on the guillotine but goes to his death with an insolent "Nuts!" to the executioner.

The story of Casque d'Or caught the popular imagination, particularly of wealthy Russians, who clamored for a glimpse of places where such crimes took place. The guides of Montparnasse were happy to oblige. "The Russians were conducted to faked *apache* dens," reported one writer. "There were the red-aproned golden-casqued girls, and the sinister-looking *apaches* with caps drawn over their eyes. In the course of the dancing, a quarrel would break out. A duel with knives would be fought. The Grand Dukes had their money's worth of thrills; and then the girls took off their aprons and the men donned respectable hats and went quietly home to bed."

The 1917 Revolution swept away Russia's aristocrats, depositing a few of them back in Paris, now as penurious waiters or doormen. Maybe they were the ones who suggested to their new employers that those faked shows still had some life in them. Cabarets adapted the knife fights into a tango called the "Apache." A girl, dressed like a whore in black stockings and a slit skirt, lets herself be scorned, rejected, and flung around the stage by a *mec* in a striped jersey, a black beret, and a look of weary contempt. In "Poor Apache," Lorenz Hart gave Chevalier a capsule description of such a performance, incorporating one of his clever rhymes.

> *While all the men are dancing*
> *Tenderly romancing*
> *I've got to throw her body around.*
> *The part that no one dares touch*
> *The spot that only chairs touch*
> *Is frequently touching the ground.*

Apache dances survived into the 1950s, long after anyone remembered their inspiration. Just after World War II, Ludwig Bemelmans, the Austrian American writer, best known for his *Madeline* books about a little Parisian schoolgirl, was taken by his friend Armand to Le Petit Balcon, a club on Passage Thiéré, near the Bastille.

> *The place was jammed. In the centre of the floor an*
> *apache was dancing wildly with his gigolette. What*

*he was doing to the girl was mayhem. He twisted
her, choked her, banged her head on the floor.
Finally a man sitting nearby jumped up in fury. He
rushed, knife in hand, at the apache—and there
was a fight and blood flowed—a pool of it appeared
on the floor. People screamed and ran. Outside, a
bus, with American Express on it, waited for them.*

*"I own a share in this place," said Armand
as the "blood" was being mopped up. "It's a gold
mine. The next show starts in half an hour. The
apache, the girl and the assassin are not allowed
to speak to anybody, because none of them speaks
a word of French. They're two ex-GI's and a girl
who used to be with a USO troupe. They all stayed
behind because they love Paris."*

32

The Gates of Night

Enter, general of the armies of the night,
at the head of your dreadful retinue.
ANDRÉ MALRAUX in his 1964 speech on the
reburial in the Panthéon of resistance hero Jean Moulin

*B*emelmans makes it seem amusing to have lived in Paris in those years after the war. Films like the 1951 *An American in Paris* reinforced the impression that the sun always shone, art flourished, and even poverty was the pretext for a joke and a song.

That idea doesn't survive long once you begin to know France. For every *American in Paris,* there's a film like *Les Portes de la Nuit—The Gates of Night*—so drenched in a sense of betrayal, despair, and shame that almost nobody in France could bear to watch. It almost destroyed the career of Marcel Carné, who, until then, had been the hero of French cinema for having made *Les Enfants du Paradis* under the occupation. Its most durable survival is the song "Feuilles Mortes"—"Autumn Leaves"—one of those hymns to despair for which the French and the Germans have no equal.

Even all these years later, the occupation is a subject best avoided. As the French say, "One shouldn't talk of rope in the house of the hanged." From time to time, however, some visitor will ask, often with a certain embarrassment, "What was it like under the Nazis?" I've taken historians on discreet tours of places in the sixth *arrondissement* that have associations with that time, but always with a sense of embarrassment, as if they'd asked me to recommend a reliable brothel.

Not long ago, the American Library asked me to interview Leslie Caron for its *Evenings with an Author* series (she'd just published a memoir). It was ironic that she'd been plucked from obscurity at nineteen to star opposite Gene Kelly in *An American in Paris*, since she'd barely lived through the war. As she describes in her book, she almost starved to death.

> *We were down to animal fodder: salsify, rutabagas, Jerusalem artichoke. . . . Fruit was as rare and expensive as tobacco. Children had one glass of milk*

a day. We were each given an ever-shrinking ration of butter; it eventually amounted to an eggcup-ful per person, per week. By the end of the war, bread was down to one slice a day per person—two-thirds flour, one-third wood shavings. Meat was also extremely scarce: about two hundred grams a week each. Cats and dogs disappeared—they were stolen and eaten. As a pharmacist, my father received cocoa butter to make suppositories, and it became the substitute for butter and oil in our cooking. Everything at our table had a faint cocoa flavour.

To keep up her strength, she was given horse blood—the horses themselves having long since been devoured.

A black market flourished, and crime with it, helped by the brownout that reduced all public lighting to half gloom. Paris was filled with refugees, deserters from the army, and prostitutes forced back onto the streets when, in a misguided attempt at social reform, brothels were made illegal in 1946 and their premises turned over to student housing.

For a lesson in how things can change, I take people to one of Paris's most popular bistros, the Balzar, just off boulevard Saint-Michel. Today, it's chic, popular, expensive, the ad hoc canteen for intellectuals from the nearby Sorbonne and Collège de France. In 1998, it was the site of a sit-in by some high-profile clients who feared changes in its style and menu after the Flo restaurant chain acquired it. All came to nothing when the Flo's CEO, Jean-Paul Bucher, dropped by to reassure them no changes would be made; why would he alter a place he'd bought because he enjoyed eating there? The waiter returned to take orders, and in a very Parisian way, political action segued into lunch.

It was a different Balzar, and another Paris, when American writer Elliot Paul ate there in the late 1940s.

We dined together at the Balzar that evening. The wind had changed direction, slightly, and there was no rain but only a different kind of chill and a sulphur-colored mist around the hooded street lamps. The brown-out had not been lifted. No lights were showing in the windows of the stores on boulevard Saint-Michel. Traffic was sluggish and sparse in the dimness. Two young men, Siamese or Filipinos, sat on a bench opposite two ratty looking girls, not prostitutes but obviously tramps. The men were dour and scowling; the girls looked bored. One of the Filipinos, or whatever he was, took from his

*side coat pocket a small automatic and laid it on
the table, looking sullenly at his girl the while. A
waiter came into the scene with a tray of drinks,
some coloured, sticky bottled appetizer. One of the
Filipinos paid the waiter; the other put the gun
back in his side coat pocket. As the waiter turned
away, the two brown men looked at one another and
suddenly smiled all over their flat round faces.*

The Balzar survived and flourished, but you can
still see signs of the old darkness. Farther up boulevard
Saint-Michel, gashes of shell fragments mark the walls of
the Ecole des Mines, the geological school and museum,
and the city is sprinkled with plaques indicating that on
this particular corner and in this gutter some *resistant* or
maquisard died for his or her country.

Of the world of Manda, Leca, and Casque d'Or, the
best reminder is Jacques Becker's romantic film *Casque
d'Or*, with young Simone Signoret as Amélie and Serge
Reggiani as Manda. But Place de la Contrescape, at the
top of rue Mouffetard, hasn't changed substantially since
Amélie, then a prostitute of nineteen, met twenty-two-
year-old Manda. (As it happens, Hemingway—that
man again—lived for a time only a few doors away,
on rue Cardinal Lemoine.) The shooting and eventual

knifing of Leca took place in les Halles, the old food and meat market, now a park to the north of rue de Rivoli. As for the Santé Prison, its walls of dark volcanic stone remain as grim as when Manda went to the guillotine.

The French stopped using the guillotine in 1977, but the Santé still retains a sinister glamour. For a while during the 1990s, its star prisoner was Ilich Ramirez Sánchez, aka Carlos the Jackal, who refused every request from the world press for an interview—except one. The editor of *L'Amateur de Cigare*, a magazine for cigar lovers, received a note, explaining, "I have just been moved, rather inopportunely, from La Santé prison. Please send all future issues of my subscription to my new residence, the isolation wing of Fresnes jail." Feeling that their shared enthusiasm gave him an edge, the editor, Louis de Torres, asked for an interview, which Carlos gave, explaining that, though "in a somewhat precarious position as far as smoking is concerned," he found consolation in reading about great cigars and recalled the summit of his smoking experiences—the opening of a box of Cuban Punch Number 13s on August 17, 1986, to celebrate the birth of his youngest daughter, Elba Rosa. As Rudyard Kipling wrote, "A woman is only a woman, but a good cigar is a *smoke*."

33

A Little Place
in the Nineteenth

*Frankly, being just plain American, I lack the
sensitivities that influence a Parisian's absolute
preference for one quarter over another, based on social
and real estate calculations that are opaque to mere
étrangers. All of Paris seems great to me.*

DIANE JOHNSON, *Into a Paris Quartier*

Occasionally, a visitor, gripped by the longing
that accompanies the end of a stay in Paris, will
ask wistfully, "How easy would it be to buy a place
here?"

"A place?"

"Oh, nothing like this." Usually they've rented a
studio apartment in one of the low-numbered *arrondisse-*

ments, an easy walk from the Louvre and the smarter restaurants. "Just a *pied à terre*."

They don't need to be more specific. I know the dream. A winding wooden staircase, worn hollow by generations of feet. The door at the head of the stairs, opening onto a neat studio; an antique bed, draped in a faded, handmade quilt found in a country *brocante*; the tiny kitchen, with milk, butter, confiture, and a baguette, still warm, on the countertop, courtesy of an obliging concierge warned of your arrival; and, of course, your own little terrace, with a view over the zinc roofs of Paris. . .

"It can't be *that* difficult, surely?" they continue. "The sixth is impossible, of course, but what about . . ." They wave in the general direction of Montmartre. "A little place—in the nineteenth, say, that just needed a bit of fixing up."

This, I think, *would be a good place to tell them about my friend Chloe.*

Parisienne born and bred, Chloe writes for one of the big weeklies.

"You've moved," I said last time we met.

"To the *dix-neuvième*. You and Marie-Do must come for dinner. When it's fixed up."

"Still working on it? But it must be, what, a year?"

"Eighteen months." She sighed. "It's a long story."

The nineteenth *arrondissement* is an old area of working-class housing. Most of us, if we see it at all, do so from the freeway, heading out of town. But Chloe and her partner Hervé thought they had found a gem. The two-story row house was one of eight on a little *allée* running off a busy suburban shopping street, close—but not too close—to Paris's outer beltway, the *périphérique*. It dated from the 1860s, as did the rough-cut stone blocks that paved the *allée*. A large basement ran under the house, and it had a tiny garden at the back.

"It looks . . . promising," Chloe told the realtor. And cheap! *Too* cheap perhaps?

"The price is negotiable," said the realtor, arousing their suspicions even more.

They understood the moment they arrived. Five cars filled every parking space.

"Clients of M. Barthelémy." The realtor indicated the butcher across the street. Apparently his clients used it as a convenient parking lot.

It got worse as they neared the house. Steps from the street led down to a basement, the door of which was wide open. Just inside, a man in dirty underpants snored on a stained mattress. An argument raged in the gloom behind him. Over all hung a reek of decay and old piss.

A quiet street in the nineteenth arrondissement

"Unfortunately," began the realtor, "you have . . ."

A girl in dirty jeans, grubby T-shirt, and bare feet came to the door, glared up at them. "If you're not looking for a fuck," she said, "fuck off," and slammed the door.

" . . . squatters," he finished.

They bought the house anyway, and petitioned the authorities to install a lockable gate across the end of the *allée*.

"As you see," said Hervé, presenting the sheaf of forms to Madame Bayard, the *arrondissement*'s *officier d'habitation*, "all residents of the *allée* are in agreement."

"Yes," she said. Her expression conveyed the wariness of someone who has learned from long experience that nothing in France happens easily. "However, an objection has been lodged."

It appeared Barthelémy the butcher wanted to hang onto his free parking lot.

"We have the right to park on our own property," protested Chloe.

"Indeed. But he claims his business would suffer if there was a gate."

"That's his problem. It doesn't give him the right to use our parking space!"

"Oh, I expect you would prevail if it went to court. But an appeal can drag on. You might like to negotiate."

A few weeks later, for €10,000, M. Barthelémy agreed not to oppose the gate, and instead to send his customers down the block, where the Champion supermarket had just built a nice new parking lot.

"Now *les squatters* . . ." said Chloe when she and Madame Bayard next met.

"We prefer *'occupants sans title.'* "

"As you wish." Chloe produced another dossier. "These list numerous complaints and arrests for drug dealing and prostitution. The people must be removed."

"The *mairie* has no right to do that. It is a matter for the police."

The *commissaire de police* could have been Madame Bayard's twin. "To get rid of these people would require a court order. And I should warn you that these are not granted lightly. There is the question of rehousing. The authorities may feel these people are less trouble on your premises than on the street."

"Can we eject them?"

"In theory, yes. But they could sue for damages if anyone is injured, or loses personal property, or is deprived of earnings."

"From selling smack. And whoring?"

"I doubt they could make that stick," the *commissaire* conceded. "But many businesses are conducted from home. They might claim to be, for instance, therapists—or financial consultants."

Chloe tried and failed to imagine clients descending into that filthy cellar for emotional or fiscal counseling.

"So we're helpless?"

"Not entirely. We can do nothing, officially. But you might like to write down this phone number."

Chloe noted the number. The *commissaire* himself didn't put his own pen to paper. Plausible deniability.

"You should have seen the guy he sent us to." Chloe lifted her shoulders and hunched her head until her neck disappeared. Her whole pose conveyed "thug." "We only ever knew him as Serge. His surname name ended in *-vitch*. All their surnames ended in *-vitch*."

"All? How many were there?"

"Eight. Big blokes—and *organized*. Obviously ex-army, probably Special Forces, but not French. Speznatz? Stasi? Belarus? Romania? Anyway, the first thing we knew, a Portakabin appeared on the main street—those prefabricated offices they put on building sites?"

"Yes . . ."

Not seeing at all. Why were Paris stories never simple?

"The next day, midmorning, Serge and his boys just . . . materialized. All in black. They marched into the basement. Four of them swept up clothes, bedding, anything portable, and transferred it in the Portakabin. Only a couple of the squatters were in the house, but they bolted, barefoot. Four more of Serge's boys stood by with new doors, steel-faced, with proper locks. It didn't take more than ten minutes to hang them. At the end, I gave Serge five thousand in cash and he handed us the keys. In two days, the stuff in the Portakabin disappeared. Then the Portakabin. We never saw the squatters again."

"And no retaliation?"

"Serge and his friends had a quiet word. That's all it needed. If you'd have seen them, you'd understand."

"But this is months ago. You still haven't moved in?"

She sighed. "Ever heard of the Law of January 17, 1992? It controls the restoration of historic buildings. It seems . . ."

But I'd stopped listening.

Chloe's story would demonstrate perfectly the drawbacks to buying an apartment. But Paris subsists on fantasy. Who was I to crush one, particularly as fragile as this. "I have spread my dreams under your feet," wrote W. B. Yeats. "Tread softly because you tread on my dreams." I'm not that cruel.

"A little place in the nineteenth? Why not? I'll keep an eye open. You never know."

❋ ·34· ❋

A Walk in Time

Last night I walked alone all over Paris, searching and
searching for miles on end. Toward two in the morning,
tumbling with fatigue down one of those empty lanes
between the Luxembourg and the boulevard
Saint-Germain, I suddenly heard the hollow tones of
wooden-heeled footsteps approaching from far behind.
I smiled to myself, slowed my pace, the feet came nearer,
growing louder, swifter. When they were nearly upon me
I shivered and was thrilled. Then the steps passed me—
but I saw no one. The regular clack of the feet walking
before me grew fainter, farther away, turned a corner
and disappeared. But I hadn't seen a soul. . .

NED ROREM, *The Paris Diary*

In most cities, it's best to stay out of alleys. Not so
in Paris, however. For one thing, *allée* in French
doesn't connote squalor and danger. An *allée*—

or *cour* or *impasse* or *pas*—can be what's called a "mews" in Britain: the courtyard behind a line of town houses where owners kept horses and carriages or, in earlier times, hunting falcons and hawks. It can even be the lane running alongside a park, lined with the sort of town houses that feature in *Architectural Digest*.

But, squalid or glamorous, all alleys have the same appeal to me. It's like going backstage in a theater and seeing the machinery that maintains the illusion. Also, it's surprising how often, while the front door of a historic building may be locked, even guarded, a door on the alley is ajar.

Everyone who visits Montparnasse walks along rue Campagne Première. Some are there to see where Jean-Paul Belmondo is shot down and expires in Jean-Luc Godard's *Au Bout de Souffle*. Others pause at number 31—the admirers of architecture pay tribute to André Arfvidson's tile-covered apartment block, a piece of secessionist Vienna transported to Paris. Others know Man Ray lived and worked here. But try cutting through the back alley picturesquely named Pas d'Enfer, the Passage of Hell, and see how Arfvidson, in those prerefrigeration days, built exterior chill cabinets into every apartment—small larders to store meat and milk, acces-

The Cour du Commerce, drawn in 1899

sible only from inside, but with a few bricks missing to allow cooling air to circulate.

At the foot of rue de l'Odéon, on a narrow island of asphalt, in front of a cinema and a café, a statue marks the former home of Georges Danton, one of the men who made the French Revolution. He stands in heroic pose, right foot forward, arm outflung. At one knee crouches a rifleman, at the other a boy with a drum. Both look up adoringly. (He appears, to tell the truth, a bit silly. John Glassco made fun of the statue: "It's the study of an angry child—a picture of outraged appeal, say to his mother over some injustice, like the theft of a toy by his elder sister. He's even pointing to her in the distance.")

Off to the right, you can just see the gates of the Abbey of the Cordeliers. The future revolutionaries, barred by the crown from renting a hall, borrowed one from the *cordeliers*—Franciscan monks who cinched their robes with cord. From 1791, they moved across the road, so I do the same, to the corner of a little one-block street called rue de l'Ancienne Comédie, because the old national theater, the Comédie Française, held its first performances there.

The Procope, where the plotters gathered in secret, is Paris's oldest café. Here the plotters coined the revolution's incendiary slogan: *"Liberté, égalité, fraternité."*

You can, if you like, take the tourist route down rue de l'Ancienne Comédie and admire the Procope's now-elegant frontage, with its display of oysters and its high-priced menu. I prefer to go round behind and, through an ancient arch, enter the Cour du Commerce Saint-André.

Yes, it looks uninviting. Walking by on boulevard Saint-Germain, you wouldn't give it a second glance. Even Danton on his plinth seems to turn up his nose. It hasn't changed much since 1732, when the Cour du Commerce was nothing but a ditch to channel storm water and worse as it rushed out of rue de l'Odéon. It still looks more like a gutter than a thoroughfare. A sidewalk clings to one edge. Ancient cobbles pave the rest, with gaps between to trap the careless high heel. Subsidence has dragged down the left-hand gutter. Buildings on that side, including the rear of the Procope, lean outward unpleasantly.

Why, then, am I drawn back to it? At least once a week, I stop walking and let people eddy around me as I stare up at the crooked roofs and attics or finger the scabbed paint and rust on a rail.

Fiction and films have taught us to see revolution in epic terms. Masses of people, usually with flaming torches, pour into plazas and besiege palaces that cover entire blocks. Speeches are made from balconies, statues toppled, treasuries looted, mansions burned. But true sedition is a secret business, plotted by a few desperate men and women in cellars at dead of night. Manifestos are composed by lamplight, behind locked doors. And printed in alleys like this.

That's how it was in 1789. The most significant events took place in an area the size of London's Soho or New York's Greenwich Village; my neighborhood, in fact. The great assault on the Bastille prison in July 14—still France's national holiday—fell flat when they found only seven prisoners inside. They burned it anyway, killed the governor, and paraded his head on a pole, but one can't escape a sense of anticlimax. Hollywood did it better. Their Bastille in *A Tale of Two Cities* was a block square, and the crowd rivaled that of the Rose Bowl.

In the Cour du Commerce, you sense what it was *really* like.

On the first building to the left, a tablet, placed almost unreadably high (out of embarrassment?), explains that on this site Dr. Joseph Ignace Guillotin, helped by a

German carpenter named Schmidt, perfected the instrument of execution that bears his name. Well, *almost* his name; an English jingle writer, finding no rhyme for "Gill-oh-tan," made it "Gill-oh-teen." Guillotin experimented on sheep; the sliding block with its angled blade is still called a *mouton*. He actually opposed the death penalty and hoped the device would be a first step in abolishing capital punishment. Instead, it encouraged fanatics like Robespierre to launch the Terror. Between sixteen thousand and forty thousand men, women, and children, from his former colleagues and friends to the royal family (and eventually Robespierre himself), fell to the machine that Guillotin promised in a burst of enthusiasm would "cut off your head in the twinkling of an eye, and you never feel it!"

Turn and look at the opposite side of the street, at the largest shop in the Cour. As I write this, it's unoccupied. It usually is. For a while it held an art gallery, then a restaurant. Between tenants, the floor-to-ceiling windows become a billboard for every concert and theatrical performance on the Left Bank. But if you find a clear spot in the glass, shade your eyes against the reflected light, and peer inside; you'll see a wall of ancient stone, and the half-cylinder of a tower buried in it. This used to house the print shop of the revolutionary Jean-Paul Marat.

The speeches of Danton and his friends arrived here so quickly the ink was still wet. His paper, *L'Ami du Peuple*, printed them, and they were carried to the banks of the Seine where *bouquinistes* sold them. Marat, plagued by a skin disease, seldom left home, but worked in a bath to relieve the itching. In July 1793, he agreed to see a twenty-five-year-old woman from Caen, Charlotte Corday, who claimed to have evidence of a conspiracy against the revolution. She stabbed him in the heart with a kitchen knife, then stood quietly waiting to be arrested. Four days after she killed Marat, Corday went to the guillotine. A year later, on March 24, 1794, Danton followed her, purged by his former friends for being, in their eyes, soft on aristos. About to be decapitated, he told the executioner, "Hold up my head afterward, where the crowd can see it. It'll be a good effect, believe me." A showman to the last.

Corday's execution also went with a flourish. As her head tumbled into the basket, Legros, a carpenter assisting the executioner, grabbed it by the hair, held it up, and slapped its cheeks. Some thought they saw a blush. An Englishwoman in the crowd swore the face "exhibited this last impression of offended modesty." It was probably just the light of the sunset striking through the trees of the Champs-Elysées, but Legros was dragged off to jail anyway. Corday, murderess or not, was no aristo but a woman of the people, and deserved to be treated with respect.

In 1892, an art student from San Francisco named Edward Cucuel rented an apartment on the Cour with his friend Bishop. His diary of their two years in Paris, illustrated with his sketches, preserves a taste of life in the Paris of Satie, Rousseau, and Apollinaire. Not that Bishop and Cucuel knew them. They were more concerned with finding the rent, hanging out with other students and models, and, from time to time, learning how to paint.

Rooms were rented unfurnished. They had to buy beds, a table and chair, even a stove, with a pipe that funneled fumes up the chimney or out the window but also provided the room with its only heat. There was no running water, and the whole building shared two squat-style toilets on the landings.

One generally couldn't cook in a studio—but one didn't need to.

Each day the street was visited by street-venders and hawkers of various comestibles, each with his or her quaint musical cry. "Voilà le bon fromage à la crème pour trois sous!" [Here's good cream

An American student cooking in his room, 1899

*cheese for three sous] cries a keen-faced little
woman, her three-wheeled cart loaded with cream
cheeses; and she gives a soup-plate full of them,
with cream poured generously over, and as she
pockets the money says "Voilà! ce que c'est bon avec
des confitures." [There you are. It's very good with
preserves.] Other women in the Cour sold bread and
rolls, hot coffee with milk, and, later in the day,
soup and stew.*

The Cour of 1892 was also a place of work.

*It had iron-workers' shops, where hot iron was
beaten into artistic lamps, grills, and bed-frames;
a tinsmith's shop; a* blanchisserie, *where our
shirts were made white and smooth by the pretty*
blanchisseuses *singing all day over their work; a
wine cellar, whose barrels were eternally blocking
one end of the passage; an embossed picture-
card factory, where two-score women, with little
hammers and steel dies, beat pictures into cards;
a furniture shop, where everything old and artistic
was sold, the Hôtel du Passage, and a book binder's
shop.*

The bookbinder survives in the boutique selling leather-bound notebooks, the bar at the end of the arcade nearest rue Saint-André des Arts still sells wine. And passing the shop selling travel souvenirs, I noticed that its stock included modern copies of antique tins from the *belle époque*, decorated with art nouveau images by Steinlen and Toulouse-Lautrec. After work, the laundresses returned to Montmartre. Some moonlighted as dancers at the Moulin Rouge, high-kicking in the can-can to show off the whiteness of their petticoats and knickers—those who wore any. And was it just coincidence that Vincente Minnelli shot some of the film *Gigi* in a side alley, the Cour de Rohan, where, behind a high green-metal gate, sometimes unlocked, a series of tree-shaded courtyards descends gently even deeper into Odéon? For more than two centuries, the Cour du Commerce has remained virtually unchanged, embedded in time. This is a place on which the past refuses to relax its grip. In a way that always escapes museums, it preserves the essence of Paris.

35

Aussie in the Métro

Dans le métro, je prends toujours des premières; dans les
secondes, je risquerais de rencontrer mes créanciers.
(On the metro, I always ride in first class. In second
class, I would risk running into my creditors.)
BONI, MARQUIS DE CASTELLANE, in the days
when the métro had first- and second-class carriages

*R*apid transit isn't noted for poetry—not in New
York or London anyway, though people speak
well of Moscow, where the underground stations are
marble: not that this necessarily makes the trains run
on time. For sheer noisomeness, it would be hard to
beat New York's subway. How insightful of Peter
Carey to describe in *His Illegal Self* "the ceiling slimed
with alien rust . . . the floor flecked and speckled with
black gum . . . [where] cars swayed and screeched,
thick teams of brutal cables showing in the windowed

dark." As for the winding, poorly sign-posted tunnels of London's Underground, with their uneven floors, one always feels as if in a rabbit run with the ferrets not far behind. Not that there might be some truth in the 1972 film *Death Line*, that a group of Victorian railway workers, walled up alive somewhere under Russell Street, might have dwindled down to a single troglodyte cannibal, preying on wandering commuters, and muttering "Mind the doors!"

What, then, is different about the Paris métro? If you've ridden it, you would not ask.

There is, for instance, the perfume. A scented antiseptic spray is applied nightly—which also explains the glossy sheen of the floors. Then there's the decor. Paris métro stations sometimes resemble women's handbags, filled with colorful but often puzzling objects, many of dubious utility. (It was a popular game in the 1920s to go through a woman's *sac à main* and analyze her character from its contents.) On any métro platform, expect to find walls covered in posters of billboard dimensions, often depicting ecstatic women wearing few, if any, clothes. Molded plastic seating in vivid pastels is standard. Likewise, vending machines for both candy and soft drinks. Some stations are decorated with mosaics, statues, or, in one case, a war memorial. Others exhibit displays in glass cases, promoting local industry or even the métro system itself, praising its efficiency, cleanliness, reliability.

And where else are platforms as elaborately decorated? Pont Neuf, nearest to *Le Monnaie*, that is, the Mint, displays old coinage and an ancient hand press. At Tuileries, tiles on one platform reproduce impressionist paintings while, on another, passengers are confronted with an illustrated time line of the twentieth century, with images of Chaplin, de Gaulle, and Josephine Baker in mid-Charleston. At Concorde, each tile bears a single letter, as if for a giant game of Scrabble. They spell out the Declaration of the Rights of Man from the 1789 manifesto of the revolution. At Varenne, nearest to the Musée Rodin, full-size replicas of his *Thinker* and statue of Honoré de Balzac rule the platform. The Arts et Metiers stop, below the Museum of Technology, imitates a submarine in honor of Jules Verne and the Nautilus of his *20,000 Leagues Under the Sea*. Copper-colored metal cladding covers the walls. The seats are of stainless steel, and there are portholes. Next to Saint-Germain and the Sorbonne, manuscripts under glass and the names of French intellectuals projected on the ceiling or eternalized in tiles remind us of France's greatest treasure, *le patrimoine*—the inheritance of the past. And on Richlieu-Drouot, an art deco memorial in black marble and gilt dating from 1931 commemorates railwaymen who died in World War I.

Louvre-Rivoli station is elaborately decorated with facsimile Egyptian statues and other antiquities. *Les taggers* caused a fuss here some years ago when they raided the station, gaudily spray-painting the tiled walls and lass cases. An initial uproar and accusations of vandalism

*One of Hector Guimard's art nouveau entrances
for the Paris métro*

gave way to a more thoughtful reaction from newspapers like the left-wing *Libération*. Wasn't graffiti also art? And didn't it deserve equal representation? The controversy continued for a few days, during which the métro authorities allowed the graffiti to remain, an object of interest to *tout Paris*, who crowded the platform to examine and discuss. Then, overnight, the spray-can art disappeared, and things returned to normal, until the next *scandale*.

In many respects, the métro is a city in its own right. We passengers become pedestrians as we negotiate the often tortuous tunnels at transfer stations like Chatelet and Montparnasse Bienvenue, where so many lines intersect that a transfer involves traveling half a kilometer, either on foot or by moving walkway. The mass of working Parisians don't regard the trip as dead time but an integral element of the day, to be enjoyed for what it can offer: a chance to read, to think, to doze, to flirt. *"Métro Boulot Dodo,"* they joke of their lives—Métro Job Sleep (which the poet Pierre Bearn expanded into *"Métro boulot bistrots mégots dodo ȝéro"*—Métro Job Café Cigarette Sleep Zero)—but the gibe is good-natured. To see a girl, a secretary or *vendeuse*, well-dressed and made up, immersed in a paperback of Kafka or Gide, is to be aware of that elegance of style and mind that has made Paris the envy of the world. In London, I've often watched women on the Underground doing their makeup on the way to work, brushing on mascara and redoing their lipstick, oblivious to the crowded carriage. In New York, many dress for the office but only from the ankles up, ruining the effect by wearing running shoes on the subway and carrying their good shoes in a bag. Parisiennes would never do either. On the métro, as anywhere outside their homes, they are on show and dress accordingly.

On a single ticket, you can ride the métro all day. (The system even has squatters, who slip in before it shuts for the night and bed down where trains are garaged at the end of the line.) You won't starve. Aside from the vending machines, there are fruit sellers at La Motte Piquet–Grenelle and a snack bar at Pont Neuf. Nor do you lack entertainment. At Châtelet, musicians tune their accordions or clarinets as they wait for the next train, then ride it for a few stops, serenading the passengers with "La Vie en Rose" or "Padam Padam Padam." Sometimes a beggar calls for attention with a formal "Excuse me, ladies and gentlemen," then gabbles his hard-luck story. His words, so often repeated he's forgotten what they mean, are nevertheless polite. Like everyone on the métro, beggars behave in a way that is *convenable*—appropriate. All is *comme il faut*—as it should be.

Given the common presence of hectic design, it was disconcerting, descending into our local métro station, Odéon, early on a winter Sunday, to find it gutted for renovation. Seating and vending machines had disappeared. Walls had been stripped not only of advertising but of tiles as well, then recemented. With nothing to reflect light from the overhead fluorescents, the tunnel became a featureless cylinder of dingy gray, relieved in its uniformity only by a single hunk of machinery, a hydraulic jack two meters long and four meters tall, supporting part of the roof. With the chilly functionality of an armed guard, it looked to have been set there like a mute sentry, to remind us that Men Were At Work, and Attention Must Be Paid.

The next man onto the near-empty platform came down the steps carrying a bunch of roses wrapped in cellophane. Fumbling in his pocket, he laid the bouquet on the only accessible horizontal space—the top of the hydraulic brace. For an instant, one almost felt he had brought them for that purpose, placing them as on an altar, in a gesture of veneration and respect. Of course the moment passed. But such a gesture would not be out of character in Paris. On anniversaries and public holidays, and thanks to a thoughtfully provided metal ring attached to the wall, a posy of flowers appears on the marble plaques all over the city that mark where someone fell during the skirmishes of the occupation. Nor had Paris's graffiti artists—*les taggers*—neglected our denuded station. The cement wall of the opposite platform was decorated (or defaced, according to taste) with a single flowingly sprayed rose.

Headed for Montmartre and lunch with a friend, I took the northern line 4, Porte d'Orléans–Porte de Clignancourt. In less than fifteen minutes, it carried me from the Left Bank, close to the city's center, to its periphery, at the foot of the hill of Montmartre that Parisians call *la butte*—the bluff.

I climbed back out into the daylight at Barbès-Rochechouart, the closest the métro approaches Montmartre. Fifteen minute ago, I'd left discreet, bookish Odéon; I emerged in what might have been Rabat or Dakar or Kabul. Black, brown, and yellow faces swirled past. Even though it was Sunday, dozens of men stood silent on the opposite corner, sheltering under the overhead railway: day laborers waiting to be hired for a few hours of heavy lifting or digging, paid, of course, *en noir*—in cash, off the books.

Edmund White came here in May 1981 to stay with friends.

A food market was set up every few days under
the elevated tracks of the métro at the Barbès-
Rochechouart stop. Piles of melons, little mountains
of saffron, cinnamon and coriander seeds, tin wells
full of various grades of couscous grains—it was a
strip of colourful Marrakesh set down in the grayest
section of the city. Just below my friends' windows
bearded old men in lace caps were selling caftans on
the street—and kids were selling drugs.

The market still exists, and the kids hanging out by the métro entrance may still sell you hash and *kif*, or at least know someone who could. To underline how little had changed, a patriarch in the hooded ankle-length robe called a *thobe* stood in front of Kentucky Fried Chicken, reflecting gravely on whether to take a tub of the regular or splurge on extra crispy.

This was a greedier Paris than my own backwater—a reef where sharks and barracuda prowled, snapping at the darting, brightly colored tourist fish. Rue de Steinkerque, barely a block long, was lined with souvenir shops selling "I ♥ Paris" T-shirts and postcards of Sacré-Coeur and the famous stone staircases, while on the street five men independently played three-card Monte, each with the same three black discs, like miniature beer mats, and three cardboard cartons, identically piled, easily toppled if the police took an interest. All used the same spiel and were watched by three apparently casual spectators, one of whom, as I passed, "won" ten euros by "spotting the lady."

A few steps farther on, a man stepped in front of me, bent, and straightened up holding a gold ring. Acting surprised, he started to ask, "M'sieur, did you lose this?" As cons go, this was even moldier than three-card Monte. I could have delivered the patter myself, since I'd heard it dozens of times—though seldom done as badly. "My religion forbids me from wearing such a ring. Also, I have no time to take it to the police or the office of Lost and Found. Why don't you keep it and give me some money now . . . ?"

I wanted to say, "If you're going to do this, at least don't let me *see* the ring roll from your hand." But who was I to tell him his business? He probably found plenty of clients among the walkers who, wearing the familiar beige windbreakers, sensible shoes, and expression of amiable wonder, wandered hand in hand, lost in the fantasy of Paris. That fantasy included dropping a few euros on three-card Monte or the ring swindle—no different than losing a few dollars in the slot machines in Las Vegas. The fun was in the game. And modern tourists, like their counterparts of the 1920s, enjoy glimpsing, however fleetingly, the larceny just below the surface of the places they visit. On bus tours of New York, drivers used to swing through the Bowery for a look at Skid Row. On the first such tour I took, a bum flung an empty bottle against the side of the bus. We all flinched as the driver explained that some locals resented being turned into tourist attractions. Some years later, I took the same tour—and jumped as an identical bottle shattered just below my window. There's no business like show business.

Paris's métro system long since took pity on the people who wilted at the multiple flights of steps leading to the pinnacle of Montmartre and installed a cable car. Its glass box lifted me comfortably to the esplanade just below the mushroomlike domes of Sacré-Coeur.

I stepped out onto a terrace which, in imagination at least, was no longer congested with men selling model Eiffel Towers and tourists snapping the view. For a moment, what Wordsworth wrote in 1802 about London in "Upon Westminster Bridge" applied no less to Paris.

> *This City now doth, like a garment, wear*
> *The beauty of the morning; silent, bare,*
> *Ships, towers, domes, theatres, and temples lie*

Open unto the fields, and to the sky;
All bright and glittering in the smokeless air.

A harpist, installed with his back to the city and well wrapped against the wind, played for a few dozen listeners seated on the steps. What was it Alice B. Toklas said? "I like a good view, but I prefer to sit with my back to it." Any angel hoping for rippling softness would have been disappointed by his music. The squared-off wooden sound box and steel strings gave it a jangling clang, a taste of Asia, reminding us that middle Europe was overrun by the Mongols, who brought with them the ancestors of those plucked and hammered stringed instruments we associate with Austria and Hungary— the zither and the cimbalom. No other tone would have suited the Spanish folk song he played. In 1952, Narciso Yepes adapted it as the theme for the film *Jeux Interdits—Forbidden Games*—a story of two children in wartime France who create their own religion of death, burying dead animals and insects in a private cemetery. For a few minutes, we who listened were no longer in France or England or Spain—just in that least national of regions, the country of the senses and the mind.

36

A Touch of Strange

Alice laughed: "There's no use trying," she
said; "one can't believe impossible things."
"I daresay you haven't had much practice," said the
Queen. "When I was younger, I always did it for half an
hour a day. Why, sometimes I've believed as many as
six impossible things before breakfast."
LEWIS CARROLL, *Alice in Wonderland*

So, tell us," said the woman from the *San Francisco Sentinel*, "what's been your *strangest* walk?"

"The *strangest* . . . ?" I said, stalling.

Strangeness has a problem; it's impossible to define. No wonder particle physicists use "strange" and "charm" to categorize the most insubstantial objects in the universe, units of energy that barely exist—at least as we know existence.

I'd found that a touch of strange added something to

my walks. Pausing in front of the old site of Shakespeare and Company, I'd point to the windows of the apartment above the shop.

"The American avant-garde composer George Antheil lived up there for a while," I'd explain. ("Avant-garde" hardly did him justice. His *Ballet Mécanique* was scored for six player pianos, two airplane propellers, four xylophones, four bass drums, and an air-raid siren.)

"Even more bizarrely," I'd continue, "Antheil and the movie star Hedy Lamarr patented a design for a remote-controlled torpedo!"

Normally nobody commented on this, except perhaps to laugh, but once it rebounded on me. The man of the couple said, unexpectedly, "Yes, it was a brilliant idea."

"You *know* about it?"

"Sure. I'm in electronics. They teach it in school. Not very practical, but clever."

The key, he explained, was Antheil's knowledge of the player piano. Using a pierced roll of paper, it can repeat a piece of music note-perfect. In the same way, a radio frequency could be made to jump every few seconds according to a code punched into the equivalent of a piano roll. Unless the enemy possessed the same roll, they couldn't jam the torpedo's frequency or send it off course.

After that, I was more cautious in my use of strange. But I still wasn't prepared for the man who knew Marlene Dietrich.

He tagged along on one of my seminar walks. Tall, about forty, with a mop of gray hair, a small, well-trimmed beard, and round steel-framed spectacles, he wore a long gray overcoat that swept to his ankles. He reminded me of Conrad Veidt in *Above Suspicion*, smiling as he demonstrated instruments of torture. His height gave him that lofty repose of men playing chess on the big outdoor boards one sees in some parks, with pieces the size of garbage cans. He seemed to look down on us, considering which to pick up between his long fingers and move to a different square.

He obviously wasn't French. But not American either. Was he even with the seminar? I never asked. It would have been . . . impolite.

As we passed the big Fnac store on rue de Rennes, I noticed a window display of Marlene Dietrich records. It was a perfect opportunity to tell a few anecdotes about my favorite actress, who, though she was born in Berlin and made her name in Hollywood, had died in Paris. But I didn't get the chance.

"I knew her, you know," a soft accented voice murmured in my ear. It was the man in the gray coat.

His use of "you know" was disturbing in its conversational intimacy. It implied we were, if not old friends, then at least well acquainted. It was that complicity I'd noticed in talking about opium, the sense of shared confidences. Except I was no longer the one sharing. With two words, this stranger had turned me from performer into spectator.

"My father was a musician," he went on. "First a pianist, then the accordion, and later a bandoleon player in a tango band. He played at La Coupole for a while. For years, they always kept a table there . . ."

The memory appeared to sadden him, since he stared for a few seconds at the enigmatic face of Marlene on the CDs, and then perked up.

"But *before* the war, he had his own band, the Moonlight Serenaders, at a hotel in Switzerland. In Basel. This is where I was born. Basel."

My group had wandered on but, seeing me in conversation with this tall stranger, straggled back. He paid them no attention, except to turn slightly to include them.

"Marlene," he continued, "would come to the hotel to meet her lover, Remarque."

Instinctively I fell into the role of straight man to this hypnotic performer. "Erich Marie Remarque. A German author," I said, for the benefit of the group. "He wrote the famous novel of the First World War, *All Quiet on the Western Front.*"

Everyone, the man included, looked at me in mild surprise. Why was I stating the obvious? I was awed at his capacity to involve us in his story. We were no longer strangers but old friends, relaxing after dinner over coffee and a *digestif.* And *of course* we knew who Remarque was.

"Remarque. Yes," he continued, picking up his thread. "He and Marlene were lovers. When she was in Europe, they would meet at the hotel. And you know, in such hotels, a guest could hire a musician, or the whole band, to play just for them. So my father and his Moonlight Serenaders were asked by Remarque to come to his suite and play while he and Marlene made love."

He looked around the group with an expression of such amiable amusement that nobody found the idea offensive, or even, it seemed, surprising. He might have been telling them that Herr Remarque liked his morning coffee black, with two lumps of sugar.

"There was a screen, you know. And my father and

his musicians sat behind it, so they could see nothing. And what is really strange . . ."

He lowered his voice conspiratorially, as if the other details had not been odd enough.

"What is strange is this. Marlene explains to my father that Remarque is able to make love in only one way. She must whisper in his ear the words of a certain song, and keep whispering them until . . . well, you know. The song is from the operetta of Franz Lehar, *Der Graf von Luxemburg—The Count of Luxembourg*. It is called 'Looking at the Stars.' So each time Marlene and Remarque are at the hotel, they request my father and his men to come to the suite, and sit behind the screen, and play 'Looking at the Stars.'"

For a moment, his attention drifted away. Was he listening to the lilt of that Lehar waltz? Then he recalled himself.

"But I am taking up your time."

Pulling back the cuff of his coat, he revealed a square gray metal watch that belonged in a museum of art deco.

"And I am sorry; I must go. But this was been most interesting. *Most* interesting."

He smiled around the group, then dived into the traffic, heading for the métro stop opposite.

Nobody commented at his departure, any more than

they showed surprise at his arrival. It wasn't unusual for us to run into other writers or artists in the street. Sometimes I invited them to pause and talk to the group. People accepted it as part of the show, proof that I really knew my city, and I didn't discourage them.

Since the sixth *arrondissement* is, in that way, a small town, I knew that the man from Basel would turn up again sooner or later. A few weeks later, I came down one morning to see him outside the bookshop opposite. He was bent over the new arrivals in the boxes along the pavement.

Coming up behind him, I said, "Anything interesting?"

He didn't look surprised. Innocently pleased, in fact.

"It is good to see you." He looked over my shoulder. "Nobody else today?"

"Not today. Occasionally I take a day off. It gives me time to do research. On *Der Graf von Luxemburg*, for example."

"Ah, really?"

"Yes. I looked it up. There's no song in it called 'Looking at the Stars.'"

"Well you know, the translators often wrote new lyrics."

"And I couldn't find the Moonlight Serenaders."

"Oh, it was a very small orchestra. And so long ago."

"But I did notice that the plot of *Der Graf von Luxemburg* does include a screen."

Such stories only exist in operetta. A penniless count agrees to marry a stranger, and to divorce her shortly after, leaving her with the title of countess so she can marry a grand duke. At the wedding, a screen separates bride and groom, to keep the ceremony completely dispassionate, so neither sees the other. Later, of course, they meet by accident and fall in love—hopelessly, as they think, not realizing they are already married.

If he noticed my implied suggestion that he'd made up the story of Dietrich and Remarque and dropped in the detail of the screen from *Der Graf von Luxemburg* to add authenticity, he didn't pick up on it.

"I'd forgotten that," he said. "But you know, such things were common around Marlene."

He turned toward me, confidingly.

"How we met is most unusual. This was when she was very old, and almost blind, and never left her apartment. Someone told me she was lonely, so I decided to make her a gift . . ."

It was a good story. Even better than the one about Remarque.

A few weeks later, a postcard arrived in the mail.

The Swiss Cultural Centre invited me to a presentation by the distinguished Swiss performance artist and playwright Hans-Peter Litscher of his newest creation. I turned the card over. On the picture side was the man from Basel, surrounded by enigmatic bric-a-brac and wearing what appeared to be a furry animal suit.

His piece was called *In Search of Eleanora Duse and Her Red-Haired Kangaroo*. You didn't know that Italy's most famous actress at the turn of the nineteenth century owned a boxing kangaroo?

Oh, it's a *very* interesting story.

❋ · 37 · ❋

The Most Beautiful
Walk in the World

Not to be rich, not to be famous, not to be mighty,
not even to be happy, but to be civilized—
that was the dream of his life.
PHILIP ROTH, *When She Was Good*

And at last we come to my own most beautiful
walk. There could only be one—down the street
on which I live, rue de l'Odéon.

I first came to it twenty years ago, when I'd just arrived in Paris and Marie-Do was pregnant with Louise.
Our daughter grew up here. I have vivid memories of
her as a toddler, briefly separated from us in a crowd,
turning to the nearest adult, a stranger, and inquiring

"Ou est Maman?"—not plaintively but with the casual confidence one employed to request directions or the time; that sureness that comes with a sense of belonging and of place.

For a book person, this was hallowed ground. I never crossed the tiled floor of our building's lobby without thinking of those who'd passed over it before me, heading up the serpentine staircase to the fourth floor.

To step onto the sidewalk of rue de l'Odéon (the first street in Paris ever to *have* a sidewalk, as it happens) was to wade into literary history. It was as if words poured in a torrent from the colonnade of the Odéon Theatre at the head of the street to boulevard Saint-Germain at its foot. In the 1700s, a few doors down the hill, printer Nicholas Bonneville lent a room to his friend, the American political writer Thomas Paine. Bonneville (and France) sheltered him while he poured out his anti-imperialist tirades, urging sedition in the American colonies with such passion that, as one hears the words, ink appears to spatter from the point of his quill like blood from a gash. "These are the times that try men's souls: The summer soldier and the sunshine patriot will, in this crisis, shrink from the service of their country; but he that stands it now, deserves the love and thanks of man and woman."

Next door, during the 1920s and 1930s, lived the American publisher and writer Robert McAlmon—christened "Robert McAlimony" after he agreed to marry a shipping magnate's Sapphic daughter, releasing her to lead a lesbian existence in Paris. With her money, he produced his modest Contact Editions. In 1923, he published three hundred copies of Hemingway's *Three Stories and Ten Poems*. The stories included "Up in Michigan," that small tragedy of a country girl's love crushed by the male world of sex, booze, and blood. "She felt Jim right through the back of the chair and she couldn't stand it and then something clicked inside of her and the feeling was warmer and softer. Jim held her tight hard against the chair and she wanted it now and Jim whispered 'Come on for a walk.'"

The book sold poorly. People found the author crude and his work worse. "The Dumb Ox," jeered snooty British modernist Percy Wyndham Lewis. Reading his review in Shakespeare and Company, Hemingway took a ruler and savagely slashed the heads off the tulips on Sylvia Beach's desk. Passing the door of the shop, now a boutique selling women's clothes, I often see those petals showering to the floor, just as I hear the querulous Dublin whine of James Joyce, half-blind and drunk on words, ranting the glorious diapason of *Ulysses*.

"Bronze by gold, Miss Douce's head by Miss Kennedy's head, over the crossblind of the Ormond bar heard the viceregal hoofs go by, ringing steel." And in the tiny apartment above the shop, Samuel Beckett and his companion, Suzanne Deschevaux-Dumesnil, hid from the Gestapo as they formed plans to flee south to safety. "I remember the maps of the Holy Land. Coloured they were. Very pretty. The Dead Sea was pale blue. The very look of it made me thirsty. That's where we'll go, I used to say, that's where we'll go for our honeymoon. We'll swim. We'll be happy."

To find your place, to share it with those you love, and to be happy—who could want more than that?

In Jacques Prévert's screenplay for *Les Enfants du Paradis*, made in the depths of the wartime occupation, the young actor Dubureau, played by Jean-Louis Barrault, stammers his admiration and desire for the lovely courtesan Garance, the greatest role of the unforgettable Arletty.

"You speak like a child," she says gently. "It's only in books that people love like that. In books and dreams."

"Dreams and life, it's the same for me," he says. "I don't care about life. I care about you."

Moved by his innocence, she says, "You're the nicest young man I've ever met." Then, "Vous me plaisez"—

Papa and Louise—
the most beautiful walk in the world

literally "You please me" but implying much more. Affection is there, anticipation, but also memory, and a knowledge that nothing lasts.

"C'est tellement simple, l'amour," she says.

It's so simple, love.

Paris, Mode d'Emploi
(Paris, A User's Guide)

"Strewth!" said a friend from Australia, contemplating his serving of *noisettes d'agneau sautées aux petits légumes* at one of Paris's more modest restaurants. "Fifty dollars for a lamb chop and veggies. Back home, you could have a whole sheep for less."

I couldn't argue with him. Paris *is* expensive—and more so every day as the pound and the dollar, U.S. and Australian, slip ever lower against the euro. On the face of it, a cheap Paris holiday seems a contradiction in terms.

Well, don't give up yet. Like most people with rural roots, the French know the value of a euro. When out-of-towners visit Paris, they don't waste a centime. Learn from them. With sensible spending and some judicious cost-cutting, you can enjoy Paris and not still be paying for it to the end of the decade.

· RULE 1 ·

Spend your money where
it does you the most good.

Is your idea of a Paris holiday lounging in a canopied bed while relays of servants deliver room-service snacks? No shame in that (if you can afford it), so by all means check into a centrally located five-star hotel, for example, the Crillon, overlooking Place de la Concorde, right next to the Champs-Elysées and the U.S. embassy—a mere $1,500 a night for a double room.

But if you're in Paris for the art, music, food, shopping, or romance, choose a three-star or even two-star establishment. They'll be off the tourist track and won't have much in the way of staff or even, in some cases, an elevator. Forget room service, too (though most offer a coffee-and-croissant breakfast). Rooms, though small, will be modern and clean, and three-star establishments will have *en suite* bathroom and toilet, telephone and TV. And you'll pay, on average, $200.

· RULE 2 ·
Eat as the French eat.

Parisian cuisine is still the best in the world—and among the most expensive. Dinner for two at the Tour d'Argent with that thrilling view of the Seine by night, or at Arpège, Paris's second-highest-rated restaurant (and one which, incredibly, uses no meat), costs, with wine, at least $1,000.

So think about breakfast and lunch.

A true French café breakfast remains one of the great pleasures of life in Paris. The coffee is fresh, the croissants, brioches, and baguettes still warm from the oven. You can eat in comfort, plan the day, and be first in line at the Musée d'Orsay or the Louvre.

Lunch is even more of a bargain. This is the "working meal" for the French, who traditionally close business deals "between the pear and the cheese." Prices average 50 percent lower than for dinner, even at the most fashionable restaurants. At Arpège, chef Alain Passard tests new creations on his lunch crowd with a set menu for less than $100. You still need to book weeks ahead, but it's worth it for his legendary *tomate aux douze saveurs*—a tomato poached in a syrup of twelve spices, served with anise ice cream.

For ordinary eating, browse the small restaurants around your hotel. Look for clients with napkins stuffed into collars, mopping their plates with pieces of baguette. The food there is almost certainly good, and cheap. Most offer a *formule* for a fixed price, with the option of either a starter or a dessert with your *plat,* or main dish. Don't be surprised if the bill comes to a little more; 15 percent service is always included, as is TVA—value-added tax, at around 19 percent of the total bill. But you can still find a good lunch, with wine, for about $40.

· SOME TIPS ·

- Don't be snobby about wine. House wines, sold by the *pichet*, or pitcher, of either 25 centiliters (two glasses) or 50 centiliters (two-thirds of a bottle), are better than you'd expect. In warm weather, try the Brouilly or other light reds, served *frais*—lightly chilled—or a Sancerre, red or white. And don't order mineral water unless you absolutely feel you need to. Just order *une carafe* and you'll get, free, what comes from the tap.

- If you're really shaving the budget, take your morning café and croissant or evening *apéritif* standing at the bar or zinc. The law limits bar prices, which must be listed on a card near the cash register. Once you sit down, the café can charge what it likes—technically for "service." And if you sit at a table outside, you'll pay still more, because the café only rents the public sidewalk from the city and passes on that charge to clients. (Incidentally, buying *un express* at the bar is the traditional quid pro quo for using the café toilets.)

- Plenty of office workers grab a *baguette fromage jambon* for lunch, and eat it while window shopping. Why be different? Shop in a supermarket and picnic on a park bench. Choose "a slice of this and a bit of that" from the delicatessen and cheese counter—it's okay to point: *vendeuses* are used to it—and a bottle from the supermarket wine section at a fraction of the price in specialist shops like Nicolas.

- Resist the inclination to tip. Every bill automatically has 15 percent service added. Even taxis. Tipping again not only wastes your money; it marks you as a *plouc*—a mug.

- Paris isn't one of those fried-egg cities, with all the interesting stuff in the middle, ringed by boring dormitory suburbs. Instead, its twenty *arrondissements* spiral out from Notre Dame, with something interesting in each of them. Think of it not as a fried egg but a soufflé, equally delectable at its crusty edges and moist center. A good restaurant, a charming hotel, an interesting museum, or an important theater can just as easily be in the twentieth *arrondissement* as in the first. Peter Brook presents his productions at Les Bouffes du Nord, a once-derelict theater in the seedy tenth. Paris's rare-book market takes place every weekend on rue Brancion in the fifteenth, in what used to be an old slaughterhouse. A little farther out is Porte de Vanves, one of Paris's best *brocantes*, or antiques markets, both more friendly and accessible than Porte de Clignancourt and infinitely cheaper.

- Use public transport. The métro is safe, clean, reliable, and cheap. So are the buses. The same tickets work for both. Buy these in a *carnet* of twelve at any métro station and you get a discount. If you're staying longer, a tourist card will cut your travel costs. Or, better still, follow the locals and get a *carte orange* at the métro station. It covers unlimited travel for a week. (PS: You'll need a passport picture.)

- Take a bike. Paris's latest way to get around is the *vélib'*—the free bike.

All over the city, you'll see racks of identical gray bikes, locked into stands, with a computer terminal at the center. To use one for a day costs just €1, and for seven days €5. Shove your credit card into the slot, receive a PIN number, and take your bike, already fitted with a basket and a lamp. When you're done, return it to any Vélib' station where there's a vacant slot.

So what's the catch?

Well, each bike is free for only the first thirty minutes. After that, you have to find another station and switch bikes or pay an additional euro for every half hour, climbing to four euros after the third hour. It keeps bikes circulating, making sure every rack is filled and nobody keeps a bike all day. But it's a bit awkward if you're a visitor taking a leisurely ride through the Bois de Boulogne and stopping for a picnic. On the other hand, imagine what a taxi would cost. And don't even *think* about renting a car.

- Plan your day, but not too much. Nothing wastes time and money more quickly than "What do you want to do today?" "I dunno; what do you want to do?" But it's almost worse to set a tight schedule that leaves no room to rest. Choose one high point—dinner at Au Bon Saint Pourcain, an ascent of the Eiffel Tower, afternoon hot chocolate at Proust's favorite café, Angelina— then improvise the rest. It's while you're walking from the métro toward the Eiffel Tower that you pass that wonderful art nouveau façade or spot the intriguing restaurant about which you'll be inducing envy in your friends back home.

- Buy *Pariscope*. This little weekly is the real Parisian's guidebook and, at less than a euro, the city's best bargain. It lists everything: movie, theater, and museum times and schedules, walking tours, auction sales, even strip clubs.

- The French eat much later than do people in other countries. Peak hour in restaurants is 8:30 to 9:00 p.m., and kitchens close around 11:00 p.m. Try booking for 7:30 p.m. The place should be quieter, the chef less frazzled, the waiters more amiable (though don't arrive too early, or you may find them eating their own dinner).

- Try going later. By day, you can queue for an hour outside I. M. Pei's glass pyramid at the Louvre and even then only see the *Mona Lisa* or the *Venus de Milo* over the heads of tour parties. But at midafternoon, the crowds melt away. Also, at 3:00 p.m. the admission price drops from €7.50 to €5, while on Wednesdays the Louvre stays open until 9:45 p.m., and not a coach party in sight.

- Paris is the world capital of souvenir shopping. However, paying boutique prices for that seductive piece of lingerie or radical kitchen gadget is the quickest way to erode your budget and load down your luggage.

  Of course browse Dior, St. Laurent, Feraud, Agnes B, and the other up-market shops in the chic quartiers around rue Bonaparte or avenue Montaigne. But then check out rue Saint-Placide, running down the side of the Bon Marché department store (the world's first, incidentally), and you may see the same items in its funkier boutiques at half the price. Key words: *Soldes*—Sale. *Promotion*—Reduced Price. *Dégriffé*—Knock-off or overstock of a known brand.

For less conventional items, visit funky ethnic districts like the Goutte d'Or (the Drop of Gold) that lap the hill of Montmartre. Shops and markets bulge with African or West Indian items. Look particularly for Moroccan brass and pottery and vivid African tribal fabrics— Yoruba, Wolof, Hausa, Mandingo.

Montmartre is also the home of Tati, Paris's favorite cheap department store for clothing, table linen, and lingerie. Madonna shopped here for those bizarre long-line bras and clunky shoes. It's worth a visit just to stare at the stock and the locals jostling for bargains. (Tati has various branches, but start with the one at 4 boulevard de Rochechouart in the eighteenth— métro Barbès-Rochechouart.)

- Forget the rules. Paris is above all a city of revelation. As Gene Kelly says in *An American in Paris*, "It reaches in and opens you wide, and you stay that way." If you want a genuinely memorable visit, embrace its extremes. For instance:
  - The Eiffel Tower stays floodlit until midnight, lighting the huge park of the Champ de Mars almost as bright as day. If the weather is

warm, take your dinner and picnic on the grass.

- Try absinthe. The modern variety lacks the alkaloid that used to rot your brain, but squint your eyes and you might even spot Modigliani or Toulouse-Lautrec. Worth a visit is Le Fée Verte—The Green Fairy, once the popular name for absinthe—at 108 rue de la Roquette, in the eleventh, near Bastille. Along with the correct art nouveau carafe to trickle water over the sugar lump into the absinthe, they also make absinthe cocktails and serve a decent late supper.

- Explore the red-light districts of Saint-Denis and Pigalle, and the hill of Montmartre above them.

- And don't miss the Musée de l'Erotisme at 71 boulevard de Clichy (eighteenth arrondissement, métro Blanche). Open from 10:00 a.m. to 2:00 a.m., its seven floors of exhibitions will give you plenty to talk about when you get home.

- But if that's too raunchy, book into Au Lapin Agile, the Frisky Rabbit, at 22 rue des Saules,

in the eighteenth arrondissement. Paris's oldest
and strangest night spot, this tumbledown
building on the untrendy north side of the
Montmartre hill was the hangout of painters
like Picasso, Vlaminck, and Maurice Utrillo,
who sneaked out the window of his mother's
house to get drunk there. For €24 you can get
a small glass of cherries preserved in brandy
and a cabaret of street songs from the time
of Renoir and Toulouse-Lautrec, performed
a capella by the house singers. Eerily
memorable.

- Then, if you think you can stand the romantic
  rush, climb the famous stone staircases of
  Montmartre around 5:00 a.m. or take the
  little cable car, buy coffee and rolls, and eat
  breakfast on the terrace below the Cathedral
  of Sacré-Coeur. If the harpist is there, drop
  a euro into his hat and ask him to play "Jeux
  Interdits."

C'est tellement simple, Paris.

BOOKS BY JOHN BAXTER

THE MOST BEAUTIFUL WALK IN THE WORLD
A Pedestrian in Paris

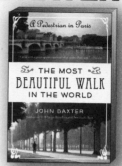

ISBN 978-0-06-199854-6 (paperback)

Walking is the best way to experience the romance, history, and off-the-beaten-path pleasures of Paris (and life itself, perhaps). In that spirit, Baxter reveals the most beautiful walks through Paris, including the favorite routes of the many brilliant artists and writers who have called the city home.

IMMOVEABLE FEAST
A Paris Christmas

ISBN 978-0-06-156233-4 (paperback)

A witty cultural and culinary education, *Immoveable Feast* is the charming, funny, and improbable tale of how a man who was raised on white bread—and didn't speak a word of French—unexpectedly ended up with the sacred duty of preparing the annual Christmas dinner for a venerable Parisian family.

WE'LL ALWAYS HAVE PARIS
Sex and Love in the City of Light

ISBN: 978-0-06-083288-9 (paperback)

For more than a century, pilgrims from all over the world seeking romance and passion have made their way to the City of Light. The seductive lure of Paris has long been irresistible to lovers, artists, epicureans, and connoisseurs of the good life. Globe-trotting film critic and writer John Baxter heard her siren song and was bewitched.